# Reflecting God's Image

Edwartheatha Long

# REFLECTING
## GOD'S IMAGE

EDNORLEATHA LONG

WESTBOW
PRESS®
A DIVISION OF THOMAS NELSON
& ZONDERVAN

WestBow Press books may be ordered through booksellers or by contacting:

WestBow Press
A Division of Thomas Nelson & Zondervan
1663 Liberty Drive
Bloomington, IN 47403
www.westbowpress.com
1 (866) 928-1240

ISBN: 978-1-5127-7773-4 (sc)
ISBN: 978-1-5127-7774-1 (hc)
ISBN: 978-1-5127-7772-7 (e)

Library of Congress Control Number: 2017903265

Print information available on the last page.

WestBow Press rev. date: 04/18/2017

This book is dedicated to the Body of Christ as they reach out in faith to reflect God's image in the earth.

Let your light so shine before men, that
they may see your good works
and glorify your Father which is in heaven.
Matthew 5:16

# Contents

# INTRODUCTION

Humans were created in the image and likeness of God with a command from God to subdue and have dominion in the earth. As God's visible representatives, they were given authority to establish the Kingdom of God in the earth realm, aligning things on earth in accordance with the heavenly blueprint. Through disobedience, that brought the infiltration of sin into the world, God's representatives failed to continue in the original command.

In spite of the disobedience which took place in the Garden of Eden, the Lord Jesus Christ, through His death and resurrection, has once again made it possible for all mankind to walk in the command of God to subdue and have dominion in the earth. Now, by grace and through faith in the redemptive work of Christ, those of faith can continue in God's original mandate to walk in authority in the earth realm.

The Lord Jesus Christ commissioned those of faith in His redemptive work to walk in *Kingdom authority* in the earth—from generation to generation. For this reason, the more those of faith (believers) understand their identity as new creatures in the Lord, the more authority they can employ to reflect the true image of God in the earth realm.

## CHAPTER ONE

# GOD'S ORIGINAL MANDATE

According to the Scripture, God created mankind to fulfill the divine purpose spoken in Genesis chapter one. God spoke His intended purpose for mankind's existence and then created them to fulfill that spoken purpose. Humans were not created without divine purpose already framed and established by the immutable Word of God. Let us take a look at God's spoken purpose for mankind's existence:

> God said, Let Us [Father, Son, and Holy Spirit] make mankind in Our image, after Our likeness, and let them have complete authority over the fish of the sea, the birds of the air, the [tame] beasts, and over all of the earth, over everything that creeps upon the earth. (Genesis 1:26 Amplified Bible)

Looking through the lens of this verse of Scripture, we understand that God made mankind to be the visible representation of the Godhead in the earth. Now, understand that this original mandate from God was not nullified or voided because of the disobedience which took place in the Garden of Eden. God's spoken Word will not return unto Him

1

nullified or void of producing what He set it in motion to accomplish. Neither Satan nor an act of the human will is powerful enough to stop the immutable spoken Word of God from the fulfillment of its purpose. In the Book of Isaiah, God testifies to the ability of His spoken Word:

> So shall My word be that goes forth from My mouth; It shall not return to Me void, But it shall accomplish what I please, And it shall prosper in the thing for which I sent it. (Isaiah 55:11 NKJV)

This divine concept governing the ability of the Word of God remains consistent throughout the written Word. How graciously God expresses this concept in Psalm 89:34,

> My covenant I will not break, nor alter the word that has gone out of My lips. (NKJV)

God highly values His Word. Psalm 138 states that He has magnified His Word even above His name.

> I will worship toward Your holy temple and praise Your name for Your loving-kindness and for Your truth and faithfulness; for You have exalted above all else Your name and Your word and You have magnified Your word above all Your name! (Psalm 138:2 Amplified Bible)

We do well to remember this truth and value it as the qualifier for God's spoken Word at work in the earth.

The concept of decreeing God's Word gives strength and credence to mankind exercising dominion in the earth realm. Mankind was to be God's portable temple in the earth with

2

the authority to release the sound of heaven into the earth realm by *decreeing* according to the spoken Word of God. In this manner, mankind would reflect the image of God in the earth realm. God's decrees, not our opinions or traditions, endure and will inevitably come into manifestation. Once again, turning to the Psalms, we gain understanding of the longevity of the Word of God.

> The sum of Your word is truth [the total of the full meaning of all Your individual precepts]; and every one of Your righteous decrees endures forever. (Psalm 119:160 Amplified Bible)

God's Word is immutable. According to Webster's Dictionary, *immutable* means "unchangeable, not capable or susceptible of change."[1] From this definition, we can say that God's word is unchangeable, not capable or susceptible of change. Also in Psalm 119, the psalmist, through the use of the phrase "forever settled," declares that God's Word is not susceptible to change:

> Forever, O Lord, Your word is settled in heaven [stands firm as the heavens]. (Psalm 119:89 Amplified Bible)

God's Word is forever settled and it has the power to bring into manifestation God's intended purpose. Therefore, we can confidently be assured that God's Word works and it will not return to Him void of the fulfillment of its purpose.

Although neither Satan nor an act of the human will could stop the original mandate God spoke over mankind, sin came in and hindered the divine mandate of God, making it necessary

---

[1] Webster's Collegiate Dictionary

for a new path of fulfillment to be revealed. I say revealed because nothing is a surprise to an omniscient omnipresent God. Although application that leads to manifestation may vary, nevertheless, God's spoken Word shall surely come to pass at its appointed time.

In addition to being immutable, God's spoken Word is holy; therefore, it must have a legal way to fulfill its purpose. Prior to the fall in the Garden of Eden, mankind's willful obedience to God's spoken Word was the holy atmosphere in which the Word worked. As this truth lubricates our spiritual eyes, we can see and understand the why of redemption. Redemption was necessary in order to give mankind a legal way back into the holy atmosphere of willful obedience to the spoken Word of God.

Redemption was necessary in order that God's spoken mandate for mankind could continue, as it had been decreed by God in Genesis 1:26, on its appointed course unto its completion.

> God said, Let Us [Father, Son, and Holy Spirit] make mankind in Our image, after Our likeness, and let them have complete authority over the fish of the see, the birds of the air, the [tame] beasts, and over all of the earth, and over everything that creeps upon the earth. (Amplified Bible)

Adam's disobedience opened a way for sin to enter into the human race. Sin marred the image of God that was housed in God's representative, Adam, causing all mankind to be off God's original blueprint. Nevertheless, sin had no power to nullify the mandate God had spoken. If mankind was to complete the course of reflecting God's image in the earth according to the original mandate, redemption would be the means. Redemption would offer everyone in the human race a legal way to be delivered from bondage to sin. Redemption would make a fresh start available to all placing faith in God's solution to sin's hindrance: the crucifixion and resurrection of Christ.

Apostle Paul tells us that God predestinated mankind to be adopted as His very own children and to be conformed into the image of Jesus Christ. Redemption provided God with the legal way to accomplish the adoptions. In this legal way provided by redemption, those exercising faith in it would become the children of God, possessing His nature in a recreated spirit. We can cross reference two passages of Scripture in order to see this truth. The first passage is in the Book of Ephesians:

> According as he hath chosen us in him before the foundation of the world, that we should be holy and without blame before him in love; having predestinated us unto the adoption of children by Jesus Christ to himself, according to the good pleasure of his will, to the praise of the glory of his grace, wherein he hath made us accepted in the beloved. In whom we have redemption through his blood, the forgiveness of sins, according to the riches of his grace. (Ephesians 1:4-7)

The second passage is in the Book of Romans:

> For whom he did foreknow, he also did predestinate to be conformed to the image of his Son, that he might be the firstborn among many brethren. Moreover whom he did predestinate, them he also called: and whom

> he called, them he also justified: and whom
> he justified, them he also glorified. (Romans
> 8:29-30)

The power of the Word of God had prevailed! Through the redemptive work of Jesus Christ, and faith in that redemptive work, mankind could return to God's original mandate. Was God's spoken mandate immutable? Yes, assuredly yes. The Apostle Peter tells us that it was not with corruptible seed that an individual is restored into relationship with God, but by the incorruptible Word of God:

> Being born again, not of corruptible seed, but
> of incorruptible, by the word of God, which
> liveth and abideth for ever. (First Peter 1:23)

Thus, we conclude that if an individual is to reflect the true image of God in the earth, the immutable Word of God must be magnified in the heart unto salvation.

## CHAPTER TWO

# GOD'S SOLUTION TO SIN'S HINDRANCE

G od wanted mankind freed from the bondage of sin and the consequences of sin so that all could have another opportunity to experience the original spoken mandate. Sin had taken mankind outside of relationship with God and hindered all humanity from fulfilling God's original mandate. Outside of relationship and fellowship with God there is no ability for anyone to fulfill God's spoken mandate. Outside of relationship and fellowship with God, life is a down spiral of immorality with no hope of moral recovery. It is written in the Scripture that all had sinned and come short of God's righteous standard.

> There is no one righteous, not even one; there is no one who understands, no one who seeks God. All have turned away, they have together become worthless; there is no one who does good, not even one. (Romans 3:10-12 NIV)

God did not create mankind to live outside of relationship with Him. God did not create mankind to live a lifestyle of hopeless immorality. God's original mandate for mankind was one of good-will whereby all would enjoy continuous fellowship with their Creator and excel in moral excellence. Therefore, God, through the death, burial, and resurrection of Jesus Christ, provided a way for everyone to return to His original mandate. Anyone can enter into that *provided way* by grace through faith in the completed work of the Lord Jesus Christ.

As the Apostle Paul takes us from the virgin birth of Jesus to the benefits derived from placing faith in His redemptive work, we can clearly see God's solution to sin's hindrance: sonship through adoption.

> But when the proper time had fully come, God sent His Son, born of a woman, born subject to [the regulations of] the Law, to purchase the freedom of (to ransom, to redeem to atone for) those who were subject to the Law, that we might be adopted and have sonship conferred upon us [and be recognized as God's sons]. (Galatians 4:4-5 Amplified Bible)

God made mankind's return to His original mandate simple and easily identifiable. He simply asked that we personally believe in the way He provided for us: the offering of Jesus Christ as the payment for the sins we had committed. Anyone who believes in God's provision for the return to relationship with Him would receive a new nature and be restored to the original mandate He decreed.

Restoration to the original mandate results in one becoming a new creature in Christ Jesus. New creatures in Christ (often referred to as believers) have the capacity to experience and distribute God's good-will in the earth realm. Becoming a new creature through faith in the redemptive work of Christ places one in a position to reflect the image of God in the earth realm. Let us take a look at the passage in the Word of God which reveals exactly what happens to anyone when he or she places faith in God's solution to sin's hindrance:

> Therefore, from now on, we regard no one according to the flesh. Even though we have known Christ according to the flesh, yet now we know Him thus no longer. Therefore, if anyone is in Christ, he is a new creature, old things have passed away; behold, all things have become new. Now all things are of God, who has reconciled us to Himself through Jesus Christ, and has given us the ministry of reconciliation, that is, that God was in Christ reconciling the world to Himself, not imputing their trespasses to them, and has committed to us the word of reconciliation. (2 Corinthians 5:16-19 NKJV)

In this passage, the Apostle Paul says, "...regard no one according to the flesh." The word *flesh* is a reference to outward behavior. As humans, we are three part beings: spirit, soul, and body. Most of the time, we ascribe an identity to a person based on their appearance (body or earthen vessel, as well as their clothing) or their actions (deeds, soul realm behavior). However, by God's standard, these things (body and soul) do not establish one's spiritual identity. Works of the flesh (soul and body) indicate behavioral patterns but not necessarily one's spiritual identity. God defines an individual's spiritual identity by the nature (spirit) contained within the earthen vessel.

In Christ Jesus, an individual's spiritual identity is defined by the nature of God that is in the recreated spirit. Since all believers possess the nature of God, their spiritual identity is *new creatures*. The old corrupt moral nature he or she possessed prior to faith in Jesus Christ is gone and has been replaced with the very nature of God, thus, Apostle Paul calls them new creatures. Let us take a look at another verse of Scripture which validates this truth.

> For He made Him who knew no sin to be sin for us, that we might become the righteousness of God in Him. (2 Corinthians 5:21)

The Apostle Paul stated that Jesus was made sin for us so that we could become the righteousness of God in Him. Those who are *in Christ Jesus* are the righteousness of God. What does this statement mean? In order to answer that question, let's take a look at the process. Those confessing faith in the redemptive work of Jesus received a recreated spirit. Dwelling in that recreated spirit is the same quality of nature as God's, often referred to as eternal life. That new nature makes believers holy and blameless before God. Consequently, every believer has the ability to stand in an upright position before God without feeling fearful, guilty, or condemned. Every believer can approach God on a friendly basis and talk with God on an intimate level of communication (as one would talk with a friend).

In John chapter fifteen, we get a glimpse of the type of fellowship believers have with the Father through the power of fellowship with the Son:

> Henceforth I call you not servants; for the servant knoweth not what his lord doeth: but I have called you friends; for all things that I have heard of my Father I have made known unto you. (John 15:15)

As new creatures, those recreated in the image and likeness of God, believers enjoy friendship with God and can now operate in dominion in the earth realm in accordance with the original mandate decreed over mankind. When believers talk and interact with others, they should view them through the new creature principle: have they believed on the Lord Jesus Christ and received a new nature. This leads us into the second revelation given in Second Corinthians 5:16-19: believers have been entrusted with the *ministry of reconciliation*. In the ministry of reconciliation, believers are to continue in the works which Jesus established while on the earth.

As we define the scope of the works believers are to do, two passages of Scripture come into view: Matthew 28:18-19 and Acts 10:38.

- According to Matthew 28:18-20, believers are commissioned to operate in the ministry of reconciliation as one of the means of exercising dominion in the earth: "...All authority has been given to Me in heaven and on earth. Go therefore and make disciples of all the nations, baptizing them in the name of the Father and of the Son and of the Holy Spirit, teaching them to observe all things that I have commanded you; and lo, I am with you always, even to the end of the Age." (NKJV)
- According to Acts 10:38, believers are to do good by destroying the works of the devil: "How God anointed Jesus of Nazareth with the Holy Spirit and with power, who went about doing good and healing all who were oppressed by the devil, for God was with Him." (NKJV). If Jesus, as the Head of the Body of Christ, was anointed to *"do good,"* the rest of His body shares that same anointing and are able to do the same good works. We

have the testimony of Christ that believers are to do even greater works than He accomplished while here in the earth realm: "I tell you the truth, anyone who has faith in me will do what I have been doing. He will do even greater things than these, because I am going to the Father. And I will do whatever you ask in my name, so that the Son may bring glory to the Father." (John 14:12-13 NIV)

Another revelation we see in Second Corinthians 5:16-19 is that believers have been given the *word of reconciliation.* With that truth in mind, let us take a look at excerpts from Peter's sermon in the Book of Acts:

> And we are witnesses of all things which He did both in the land of the Jews and in Jerusalem, whom they killed by hanging on a tree. Him God raised up on the third day, and showed Him openly, not to all the people, but to witnesses chosen before by God, even to us who ate and drank with Him after He arose from the dead. And He commanded us to preach to the people, and to testify that it is He who was ordained by God to be Judge of the living and the dead. To Him all the prophets witness that, through His name, whoever believes in Him will receive remission of sins. (Acts 10:39-43 NKJV)

Although this sermon contains many divine truths, there are three truths we want to highlight and study in order to gain insight into the *word of reconciliation* we have been given to proclaim to others:

❖ The statement, *"whom they killed by hanging on a tree,"* is the proof that believers have been redeemed from the curse of breaking the law. Galatians 3:13 states, "Christ hath redeemed us from the curse of the law, being made a curse for us: for it is written, Cursed is every one that hangeth on a tree." The eternal truth that Jesus hung on a tree taking the curse for us is the believer's legal ground for the release from sickness or anything else written in the curse of the law. The curse of the law is listed in the latter half of Deuteronomy chapter twenty-eight, which basically states that violators of the laws of God will never be healed, never be successful, and would die of sickness or disease. Although Galatians 3:13 specifically states that Christ took the curse and opened the way for us to receive blessings from God, some believers choose to continue walking in the age old *"never be anything but a victim"* mentality every day. This is partially due to the distorted image of self and God that some believers embrace as their Kingdom reality. Unfortunately, some have embraced distorted images of self and God because of lack of discipleship. Regardless of how distorted their images may be, the eternal reality that Jesus was made a curse for us so that God would have a legal way to bless us does not change! God wants to see us prosper and be in good health even as our souls prosper. What a powerful word of reconciliation this eternal truth is to those of faith in God's solution to sin's hindrance: God wants to see us prosper. By the crucifixion of Jesus Christ, the old account that kept us an enemy to God has been paid in full and moved out of the way of hindering relationship with God. Hallelujah and Amen. First Corinthians 5:7 tells us that Christ, as our Passover Lamb, made redemption a legal reality for all who believe in His substitutionary work on the cross. Because Christ by His own blood ransomed us from the kingdom of darkness, all who believe have a legal right to relationship with God and their faculties (spirit, soul, and body) belong to God. Those of faith in the substitutionary work of Jesus are no longer the property of the devil but now belong to God. The adversary no longer has any legal right to those who have accepted the eternal truth of redemption as their reality.

❖ *Jesus is alive is the second eternal truth we want to take into consideration.* Unlike other religions, Christianity is a relationship with a living Savior: the Lord Jesus Christ. Jesus is alive and declared to be the Son of God by the testimony of the Holy Spirit who raised Him from the dead (Romans 1:4). Jesus is alive and seated at the right hand of the Father, far above any power of evil in this world and in the world to come (Ephesians 1:20, Hebrews 10:12). Jesus is alive and is the universal head of the Church called the body of believers (Ephesians 1:22-23). Since Jesus is alive, there is no need of another prophet to speak for God as Jesus is the living word of God's revelation and the final word of God the Father to mankind. Any prophetic voice declaring authority to speak to the people must be sent by the Son. From the Mount of Transfiguration, the voice of the Father validates this truth: "This is my beloved Son, in whom I am well pleased; hear ye him." (Matthew 17:5) Also the Book of Hebrews validates that God is speaking to mankind through His Son Jesus Christ. Hebrews 1:1-2 states, "God, Who at sundry times and in divers manners spake in time past unto the fathers by the prophets, hath in these last days spoken unto us by his Son, whom he hath appointed heir of all things, by whom also he made the worlds." In the governmental structure of the Kingdom of God, it is the Son who sends prophets to declare the Kingdom of God to mankind (Ephesians 4:11).

❖ *We must believe in order to receive is a foundational Kingdom principle of faith that we cannot overlook.* Faith is the language of the Kingdom of God and the faith walk or active faith is the only acceptable way to reflect God's image in the earth. God created mankind with an ability to walk in two realms: earth and spirit. It takes active faith to enter into the spirit realm and communicate with God. Without active faith it is impossible to comprehend God's existence and character. The act of believing that God exists and that He is a rewarder of those who diligently seek Him is faith in action or what is referred to as active faith (Hebrews 11:6). Active faith is necessary in order to operate in the dominion mandate spoken by God at the creation of mankind. Active faith is the evidence that one is not just hearing the Word of God, but putting the Word to work in the life. Active faith is necessary to receive the manifestation of the promises of God. Hebrews 4:2 states that Israel did not receive what was promised because they did not mix faith with the Gospel message they heard. In the Kingdom of God, faith is to be the lifestyle of every believer from start to finish: believers were justified by faith (Romans 5:1), have access into the grace of God by faith (Romans 5:2), daily live by faith (2 Corinthians 5:7, Galatians 3:11, Hebrews 10:38), move forward in the bold assurance of faith (Hebrews 10:22), and grow from faith to faith (Romans 1:17). Faith helps us to penetrate areas of unbelief and bring them captive to the Word of God in order to move forward into trusting in the goodness of God—He is the reward of those walking in faith.

The word of reconciliation which we share with others honors the goodness and kindness of God and portrays Jesus as our living Savior and Lord. A brief summary of the word of reconciliation may be stated as follows: God is not angry with mankind, but loved us so much that He sent Jesus to make a way for everyone to come back into relationship with Him and experience His presence. To enter into God's made way of coming back into relationship with Him, one need only to repent of sin and believe on Jesus Christ as the one who gave His life as the payment for our sins. A payment we know was accepted by God and works on our behalf because the Holy Spirit raised Jesus from death: Jesus is alive, sitting at the right hand of the Father and praying for each one of us—He is alive.

If mankind is to reflect God's image and exercise dominion in the earth, placing personal faith in the redemptive work of Jesus Christ for the forgiveness of sin, the acceptance of that forgiveness and continuous unbroken fellowship with a risen Savior is necessary—without option. In order for mankind to return to the original mandate, salvation must take place first: individuals must repent and accept God's forgiveness of sin. Once an individual returns to the original mandate by becoming a believer, continuous fellowship with a living Savior gives the boldness needful to exercise dominion and reflect God's image in the earth realm. Continuous fellowship with a living *risen Savior* is made possible by the ministry of the Holy Spirit. If those of faith acknowledge and yield to the ministry of the Holy Spirit, just as Jesus did in Acts 10:38, there will be no hindrances to reflecting God's image in the earth.

## CHAPTER THREE

# NEW CREATURE'S TRUTHS

As a result of God's nature at work in those of faith, there are new creature's truths (benefits) believers are to experience. One of the benefits is the restoration of fellowship. Receiving God's nature restored believers' capacity to fellowship with God the Father and with His Son, Jesus Christ, at a level of intimate communication. The Father and the Son become an increasing reality to believers who utilize the capacity of intimate fellowship. Due to the lack of knowledge of this truth, not all believers utilize this capacity. Nevertheless, the Apostle John states that a distinguishing mark of those of faith is fellowship with the Father and with the Son. This distinguishing mark of fellowship with a living God makes Christianity far above any religion because none of their gods are alive.

> What we have seen and [ourselves] heard, we are also telling you, so that you too may realize and enjoy fellowship as partners and partakers with us. And [this] fellowship that we have [which is a distinguishing mark of Christians] is with the Father and with His

Son Jesus Christ (the Messiah). (First John 1:3 Amplified Bible)

The God worshiped in Christianity is alive! The God of Christianity is not a carved image but an eternal living being. It is a living Jesus who promised that He and the Father would commune with believers at a revelatory level.

> The person who has My commands and keeps them is the one who [really] loves Me; and whoever [really] loves Me will be loved by My Father, and I [too] will love him and will show (reveal, manifest) Myself to him. [I will let Myself be clearly seen by him and make Myself real to him]. (John 14:21 Amplified Bible)

Before the fall in the Garden of Eden, Adam and Eve (God's representatives) possessed the capacity to intimately commune with God. Because Adam represented mankind, his disobedience to God's command caused a deadly disease to infest all humankind. That deadly disease was sin. Adam's disobedience opened a way for sin to shut the door to the capacity of intimate fellowship with God.

Disobedient Adam had fallen from his original position of intimate fellowship with God and lacked the ability to return. Sin affected every faculty and took mankind to a level of depravity that left everyone with an inability to readily embrace the truth of God's existence as their Creator. Adam's fallen condition left mankind in need of forgiveness of sin and restoration to God's original mandate. Humans did not pursue their Creator, but continuously engaged in immorality. It was because of God's great love for mankind that He pursued fellowship with fallen mankind. The greatest expression of

God's love for mankind was the giving of Jesus Christ as the payment for our sins.

> For God so loved the world, that he gave his only begotten Son, that whosoever believeth in him should not perish, but have everlasting life. (John 3:16)
>
> But God commendeth his love toward us, in that, while we were yet sinners, Christ died for us. Much more than, being now justified by his blood, we shall be saved from wrath through him. (Romans 5:8-9)

Jesus came into this world to be God's sacrificial lamb. The offering of Jesus, as the sacrifice needful to pay for mankind's sins, removed the partition of enmity between mankind and God and gave mankind a road back to fellowship with God. Whosoever exercises faith in this truth enters into the new birth experience and receives the restored capacity to intimately fellowship with God through the shed blood of Jesus Christ. The Book of Hebrews tells us that Christ offered His own blood so that we could have a way back to fellowship with God.

> Under the old system, the blood of goats and bulls and the ashes of a young cow could cleanse people's bodies from ritual defilement. Just think how much more the blood of Christ will purify our hearts from deeds that lead to death so that we can worship the living God. For by the power of the eternal Spirit, Christ offered himself to God as a perfect sacrifice for our sins. (Hebrews 9:13-14 NLT)

Through the new birth, those of faith receive forgiveness of sin and the capacity to return to fellowship with the Father through the Son. Consequently, as the Holy Spirit works through each believer's new birth experience, believers are able to effectively exercise the restored spiritual capacity, grow into maturity, and reflect the true image of God in the earth.

Several other benefits which are available to believers because of the restored capacity are: (1) ability to respond to the love of God, (2) ability to personally know God as Father, (3) ability to receive revelation knowledge, and (4) ability to walk in obedience to God's commands. From New Testament, let us take a look at these benefits of the restored capacity.

## Ability to Respond to the Love of God

Responding to the love of God is vital to the ability to trust God, exercise faith, and walk free of orphan mentality. The Apostle John gives us several instructions that will help us understand the love of God at work in our restored spiritual capacity or new nature:

> Anyone who confesses (acknowledges, owns) that Jesus is the Son of God, God abides (lives, makes His home) in him and he [abides, lives, makes his home] in God. And we know (understand, recognize, are conscious of, by observation and by experience) and believe (adhere to and put faith in and rely on) the love God cherishes for us. God is love, and he who dwells and continues in love dwells and continues in God, and God dwells and continues in him. In this [union and communion with Him] love is brought to completion and

attains perfection with us, that we may have confidence for the day of judgment [with assurance and boldness to face Him], because as He is, so are we in this world. (1 John 4:15-17 Amplified Bible)

The first truth embedded in this passage is that only believers, those who confess that Jesus is the Son of God and the ransom for our sins, possess the God-kind of love. The next truth we can embrace is as God lives and makes His home in believers, we can "understand, recognize, are conscious of, by observation and by experience," the God-kind of love. Simply stated, as God lives in us and we live in Him, His love-ways become clear to us. Only those who continue in "union and communion with Him" are perfected in the God-kind of love is the third truth contained within this passage. As believers commune with God, their attitudes change and become more like His, and they move away from the enemy of faith, which is fear.

There is no fear in love [dread does not exist], but full-grown (complete, perfect) love turns fear out of doors and expels every trace of terror! For fear brings with it the thought of punishment, and [so] he who is afraid has not reached the full maturity of love [is not yet grown into love's complete perfection]. (1 John 4:18 Amplified Bible)

The goal of the God-kind of love is to bring those of faith into a place of maturity whereby they can experience the goodness of God and walk free of bondage to fear. Fear is not a part of God's original design for mankind. Fear came when sin entered into the human race through Adam's disobedience in the Garden of Eden. Thus, operating in fear is the evidence that the original sin-consciousness inherited from Adam's disobedience is dominating the heart and that the God-kind of love has not been allowed to influence the heart. When believers commune with the Holy Spirit, and exercise obedience to His guidance, fear is "turned out of doors" and every trace of terror expelled; the God-kind of love dominates the heart and faith, which works by the God-kind of love, reaches full maturity.

The Apostle John also told us that believers love God because He first loved us, and we can reflect that love to others, if indeed the God-kind of love is really in us.

> We love Him, because He first loved us. If anyone says, I love God, and hates (detests, abominates) his brother [in Christ], he is a liar; for he who does not love his brother, whom he has seen, cannot love God, Whom he has not seen. And this command (charge, order, injunction) we have from Him: that he who loves God shall love his brother [believer] also. (1 John 4:19-21)

In order to reflect God's image in the earth realm, the God-kind of love must prevail in every area of the believer's life. All hypocrisy, prejudices, racism, and the like must not be found in the household of faith. God's love in us is pure! Thus, as we interact with others, our attitudes must be free of any contaminations which would hinder the flow of that pure love. The greatest witness to the reality of God's existence is found in the God-kind of love which believers have for each other. One of the biggest weapons the enemy uses to mar the love-image of God is racism. Through humility and cooperating with the grace of God, this tool of the enemy can be turned out of doors and destroyed. The command is "he who loves God shall love his brother [believer] also." If your desire is to reflect the true image of God in the earth, the command to live the God-kind of love lifestyle will have to be obeyed.

## Ability to Personally Know God as Father

In order to reflect the image of God as a loving Father, believers will have to yield steadfastly to the ministry of the Holy Spirit as He brings the assurance of God's love and trains the heart to cry out *"Abba, Father."* Only through obedience to the ministry of the Holy Spirit will believers walk free of the spirit of fear and orphan mentality which mar the true image of God in the heart and mind.

> For [the Spirit which] you have now received [is] not a spirit of slavery to put you once more in bondage to fear, but you have received the Spirit of adoption [the Spirit] producing sonship] in [the bliss of] which we cry, Abba (Father)! Father! (Romans 8:15 Amplified Bible)

From this passage, we can clearly see that operating in the spirit of fear denotes sin consciousness and bondage. Operating in bondage to fear is the evidence that believers are not communing with the Holy Spirit at sonship level. Endeavoring to live free of bondage to fear without knowledge and understanding of the Holy Spirit's ministry is like trying to drive a car with a flat tire—it will be a hard difficult journey.

Jesus promised not to leave those of faith as orphans, but to send the Holy Spirit to be with us.

Jesus kept His word and sent the Holy Spirit to abide in us forever.

> And I will ask the Father, and He will give you another Comforter (Counselor, Helper, Intercessor, Advocate, Strengthener, and Standby), that He may remain with you forever—The Spirit of Truth, Whom the world cannot receive (welcome, take to its heart), because it does not see Him or know and recognize Him. But you know and recognize Him, for He lives with you [constantly] and will be in you. I will not leave you as orphans [comfortless, desolate, bereaved, forlorn, helpless], I will come [back] to you. Just a little while now, and the world will not see Me any more, but you will see Me; because I live, you will live also. At that time [when the day comes] you will know [for yourselves] that I am in My Father, and you [are] in Me, and I [am] in you. (John 14:16-20 Amplified Bible)

For many years, the Holy Spirit was erroneously looked upon as some spiritual force that caused individuals to behave uncontrollably. In these last days, God has commissioned excellent teachers in the Body of Christ who continue to expose and dispel these erroneous teachings. Now, because of these excellent teachers, there are many believers who honor and respect the person of the Holy Spirit and yield to His ministry.

Before the salvation experience, all believers were alienated from God and operated in orphan mentality. Since no believer had experienced Kingdom living prior to salvation, the laws governing Kingdom citizenship must be learned. One of those laws is experiencing and expressing the God-kind of love. The God-kind of love (agape`) is the nature of God that is at work in every believer, helping believers to stay away from orphan mentality in order to walk in their citizenship rights. The God-kind of love has been poured out in the hearts of believers by the ministry of the Holy Spirit.

> Such hope never disappoints or deludes or shames us, for God's love has been poured out in our hearts through the Holy Spirit Who has been given to us. (Romans 5:5 Amplified Bible).

The degree to which the God-kind of love influences the lives of believers depends on how yielded the individual is to the ministry of the Holy Spirit. The old familiar habits of the flesh (carnal nature) will want to continue their role of domination in the life of every believer. However, if believers allow the Holy Spirit to guide the heart, He will help each believer to mortify the old ways of responding and train each yielded believer how to respond with the God-kind of love.

> So then, brethren, we are debtors, but not to the flesh [we are not obligated to our carnal nature], to live [a life ruled by the standards set up by the dictates] of the flesh. For if you live according to [the dictates of] the flesh, you will surely die. But if through the power of the [Holy] Spirit you are [habitually] putting to death (making extinct, deadening) the [evil] deeds prompted by the body, you shall [really and genuinely] live forever. For all who are led by the Spirit of God are sons of God. (Romans 8:12-14 Amplified Bible)

When believers operate in the God-kind of love, their lives escalate to the failure-proof zone. This statement simply means that believers have an answer for every situation because the wisdom of God is constantly available to them. First Corinthians 13:4-8 describes the nature of the God-kind of love in believers as: "Love suffers long and is kind; love does not envy; love does not parade itself, is not puffed up; does not behave rudely, does not seek its own, is not provoked, thinks no evil; does not rejoice in iniquity, but rejoices in the truth; bears all things, believes all things, hopes all things, endures all things. Love never fails."

## Ability to Receive Revelation Knowledge

Receiving revelation knowledge is the bedrock to believers operating in power and authority in the earth. Concerning the doctrines and principles of the Kingdom of God, believers are not to voice personal opinions or teach their opinions to others, but they are to receive revelatory knowledge and teach by the wisdom of the Spirit. We see this truth demonstrated in the life of Jesus while He ministered in the earth.

> I have many things to say and to judge concerning you, but He who sent Me is true; and I speak to the world those things which I heard from Him." (John 8:26 NKJV)

We know that our lives are to be governed in like manner because the Lord informed the disciples that their ability to hear and understand would increase once they availed themselves of the ministry of the Holy Spirit.

> I still have many things to say to you, but you cannot bear them now. However, when He the Spirit of truth, has come, He will guide you into all truth; for He will not speak on His own authority, but whatever He hears He will

speak; and He will tell you things to come."
(John 16:12-13 NKJV)

The Apostle Paul made a wholehearted commitment not
to teach his opinions to the people so that their faith would
not rest on human opinions.

> And my speech and my preaching was not
> with enticing words of man's wisdom, but in
> demonstration of the Spirit and of power; that
> your faith should not stand in the wisdom
> of men, but in the power of God. Howbeit we
> speak wisdom among them that are perfect:
> yet not the wisdom of this world, nor of the
> princes of this world, that come to nought:
> But we speak the wisdom of God in a mystery,
> even the hidden wisdom, which God ordained
> before the world unto our glory. (1 Corinthians
> 2:4-7)

It pleases God to reveal the Kingdom of God to His children;
therefore, the *mysteries* of the Kingdom are simply hidden
revelations *reserved* to be given in the form of revelation
knowledge to those of faith.

> [Things are hidden temporarily only as a
> means to revelation.] For there is nothing
> hidden except to be revealed, nor is anything
> [temporarily] kept secret except in order that
> it may be made known. If any man has ears to
> hear, let him be listening and let him perceive
> and comprehend. (Mark 4:22-23 Amplified
> Bible)

In the teaching about the parable of the sower, Jesus told the disciples that revelation knowledge of the Kingdom of God would be given to those who want to know the truth. The religious leaders were not seeking truth, but a means to expose Jesus as a heretic so the meaning of the parable was not given to them. However, this was not the case with the disciples. Jesus' disciples were genuinely hungry to learn about the Kingdom of God. Therefore, Jesus explained the meaning of the parable to the disciples and assured their hearts that God had purposed for His children to know and understand the economy of the Kingdom.

> He who has ears [to hear], let him be listening and let him consider and perceive and comprehend by hearing. Then the disciples came to Him and said, Why do you speak to them in parables? And He replied to them, To you it has been given to know the secrets and mysteries of the kingdom of heaven, but to them it has not been given. (Matthew 13:9-11 Amplified Bible)

Is your motive right as you seek to understand the mysteries of the Kingdom of God? It is a biblical truth that revelation knowledge about the Kingdom of God is given to all who are genuinely hungry for reality as God sees it—those who are hungry for truth. It is the Father's good pleasure to satisfy these hungry souls by revealing the mysteries of the Kingdom of God to them.

## Ability to Obey the Commands of God

Walking in obedience to the commands of God is as vital to experiencing the new creature's truths as natural air is to the maintaining of physical life. Obedience to God is the only way to operate in the Kingdom mandate to have dominion in the earth. When Adam failed to operate in obedience to God, he lost his right to operate in dominion in the earth. The *obedience to God principle* was demonstrated by Jesus as He exercised the right to establish Kingdom authority in the earth realm. This same Jesus tells us how important it is to operate in obedience in order to have dominion in the earth.

> If you live in Me [abide vitally united to Me] and My words remain in you and continues to live in your hearts, ask whatever you will, and it shall be done for you. (John 15:7 Amplified)

Making a commitment to walk in obedience to the Father's will is not optional, especially for those in the household of faith. In addition to not being optional, it is a quality decision that comes with great reward. Once again, Jesus is our example of making a commitment to walk in obedience to the Father's will and receiving a great reward because of that commitment. In the Kingdom of God, Jesus is the centerpiece of praise. This position of honor was bestowed upon Him because of His obedience to the Father. Those in the household of faith are to imitate this same type of obedience to the will of the Father through obedience to the Son. The Apostle Peter says that believers have been sanctified unto obedience to Jesus Christ.

> Who were chosen and foreknown by God the Father and consecrated (sanctified, made holy) by the Spirit to be obedient to Jesus Christ (the Messiah) and to be sprinkled with [His] blood: May grace (spiritual blessing) and peace be given you in increasing abundance [that

spiritual peace to be realized in and through Christ, freedom from fears, agitating passions, and moral conflicts]. (1 Peter 1:2)

The Kingdom of God is not a *"bless my four and no more club."* This Kingdom is about fulfilling the Father's will in the earth realm. This truth comes into view in the prayer Jesus taught the disciples to pray.

Pray, therefore, like this: Our Father Who is in heaven, hallowed (kept holy) be Your name. Your kingdom come, Your will be done on earth as it is in heaven. (Matthew 6:9-10 Amplified Bible)

As believers honor God as Father by giving Him the holy reverence due His name, the heart will quickly surrender to doing His will in the earth. Always remember that impure motives, such as seeking to gain a reputation for self, will not surrender to obeying the Father's commands.

I'm not sure of the origin of the teaching that believers don't have to walk in obedience to the commands of God, but just live by grace; however, it has become quite obvious that those teaching that doctrine have little understanding of the goal and ability of grace. God sends grace to give believers the ability to walk in obedience to His commands. Notice that the Apostle Peter understood the correlation between the two and acknowledged that God the Father made us holy for the purpose of being obedient to Christ. Peter, understanding the goal and the power of grace, prayed for grace, as well as peace, to be given in abundance.

Where there is sin in the life, grace has the ability to separate those of faith in God's ability from sin's dominion and deliver them into the Kingdom of God. Grace, God's ability and unmerited favor, is the basis of all believers' freedom from moral decay. Although some religions claim to know the road to moral freedom and eternal happiness, the truth is no human ability can free humanity from the bondage of sin. Only by faith working through grace, the ability and unmerited favor of God, is freedom (deliverance) made possible. See and understand that all God has to offer mankind comes by faith through God's favor and ability: the free gift of grace. The Apostle Paul plainly states this truth in the Book of Romans:

> [All] are justified and made upright and in right standing with God, freely and gratuitously by His grace (His unmerited favor and mercy), through the redemption which is [provided] in Christ Jesus, Whom God put forward [before the eyes of all] as a mercy seat and propitiation by His blood [the cleansing and life-giving sacrifice of atonement and reconciliation, to be received] through faith. (Romans 3:24-25a Amplified Bible).

Grace is the only ability that helps believers to reflect the true image of God in the earth. Without the power of grace at work in the lives of believers, all is a work of the flesh and an unacceptable offering unto God.

The Word of God declares that God gives more grace to anyone who has humbled the heart to understand the need for it operating in the life.

> But He gives us more and more grace (power of the Holy Spirit, to meet this evil tendency and all others fully). That is why He says, God sets Himself against the proud and haughty, but gives grace [continually] to the lowly (those

who are humble enough to receive it). (James 4:6 Amplified Bible)

Individuals operating in immorality, yet claiming to live by grace, are not telling the truth. As the goal of grace is to lift one out of sin and into the presence of God, it is never a stagnant gift but a trainer which teaches one to live holy and in intimate fellowship with God. We can cross reference two passages of Scripture to verify the ability of grace:

So let us come boldly to the throne of our gracious God. There we will receive his mercy, and we will find grace to help us when we need it. (Hebrews 4:16 NLT)

For the grace of God (his unmerited favor and blessing) has come forward (appeared) for the deliverance from sin and the eternal salvation for all mankind. It has trained us to reject and renounce all ungodliness (irreligion) and worldly (passionate) desires, to live discreet (temperate, self-controlled), upright, devout (spiritually whole) lives in this present world. (Titus 2:11-12 Amplified Bible).

Once again, grace, God's unmerited ability and favor at work in believers, trains us to live holy.

## CHAPTER FOUR

# THE WALK OF FAITH

The Kingdom of God is not governed by temporal circumstances or our five senses. It is a spiritual Kingdom governed by eternal laws which create, establish, sustain, uproot, remove, and restore. One of those eternal laws is the law of faith. In order to reflect God's image in the earth, believers will have to learn to walk (live) by the law of faith and not by sense knowledge. Believers' everyday practical living must be regulated by faith. The Amplified Bible gives an excellent explanation of walking by faith:

> For we walk by faith [we regulate our lives and conduct ourselves by our conviction or belief respecting man's relationship to God and divine things, with trust and holy fervor; thus we walk] not by sight or appearance. (2 Corinthians 5:7 Amplified Bible)

The Word of God declares that the justified, those individuals who have been made just as if they had never sinned, live by faith. God expects believers not to allow the heart to be governed by fear and agitation, but to operate by faith and to grow in faith.

> But the just shall live by faith [My righteous servant shall live by his conviction respecting man's relationship to God and divine things, and holy fervor born of faith and conjoined with it]; and if he draws back and shrinks in fear, My soul has no delight or pleasure in him. (Hebrews 10:38 Amplified Bible)

Now, since we understand that faith is an essential Kingdom principle, and if we are to reflect God's image in the earth, we must operate by the law of faith, let us take a look at the biblical meaning of faith. From the pages of the Amplified Bible, we find several working definitions for the word, *faith*.

> Remember your leaders and superiors in authority [for it was they] who brought to you the Word of God. Observe attentively and consider their manner of living (the outcome of their well-spent lives) and imitate their faith (their conviction that God exists and is the Creator and Ruler of all things, the Provider and Bestower of eternal salvation through Christ, and their leaning of the entire human personality on God in absolute trust and confidence in His power, wisdom, and goodness). (Hebrews 13:7 Amplified Bible)

From the statement, "their conviction that God exists and is the Creator and Ruler of all things, the Provider and Bestower of eternal salvation through Christ," we learn that faith is a *conviction* that honors God's existence, sovereign rulership, and gracious gift of His Son Jesus Christ as the Redeemer. Also, we see that faith encompasses trusting God with the whole of one's personality. The faith that pleases God is active and not passive. It involves the leaning of the entire human personality on God in absolute trust and confidence in His power, wisdom, and goodness. Believing and confidently trusting in God's power, wisdom, and goodness is the evidence that one is operating in active faith. Here are several points to remember about faith:

- Faith confidently trusts that God is more powerful than any foe, whether the foe is natural or spiritual. This was David's testimony when he approached Goliath; consequently, Goliath's defeat was inevitable.
- Faith does not lean toward human understanding, but confidently trust in the counsel of God and listens to obey His voice.
- Faith confidently trusts that God is good and not evil. Therefore, those operating in faith are fully persuaded that God's plan for the worshiper's life is one of success and not of failure.

From another passage in the Amplified Bible, we understand that faith equips believers with an *ability to see beyond natural circumstances* while helping believers to operate effectively in two realms: physical and spiritual.

> Now faith is the assurance (the confirmation, the title deed) of the things [we] hope for, being the proof of things [we] do not see and the conviction of their reality [faith perceiving as real fact what is not revealed to the senses]. (Hebrews 11:1 Amplified Bible)

Faith sees the invisible realm of God's domain and operates by the laws of that realm. Faith testifies of God's reality and Kingdom authority to change what the natural eyes behold.

It is this ability of faith that helps believers effectively reflect God's image in the earth realm.

God created mankind with the capacity to operate in both the spiritual and physical realms. Mankind was created to walk in the spirit and rule the physical world through spiritual mandates and spoken decrees. The word *walk* means how one's lifestyle is governed or the manner of conduct employed. God made human beings a little lower than Himself (Psalm 8:5), creating in mankind the ability to release heavenly government into the earth realm through spoken decrees. Humans were created with the ability to walk (govern the lifestyle) by faith and not by physical sight. It was this ability that gave credence to the mandate to subdue and have dominion in the earth. Until their fall in the Garden of Eden, faith and divine wisdom prevailed in mankind's spiritual eyes and understanding. The very moment Adam and Eve allowed their physical senses to dictate their lifestyle their original position with God was lost. Nevertheless, those who enter into relationship with God regain the ability to walk by faith and not by sight. After the initiation of restoration to God's original divine order for mankind, every believer's responsibility is to choose to live continuously by faith rather than by the impulses of the five senses.

Faith gives the ability to live in an entirely new way. Such was the case with many of the patriarchs and matriarchs of the Old Testament who entered into a covenant relationship with God. For example, Abraham, choosing to walk by faith, received the manifestation of God's promise that he and his wife, Sarah, would have a son (Genesis 21:1-7). When God tested Abraham in Genesis chapter 22, Abraham spoke through the eyes of faith concerning the ending results of offering Isaac as a burnt offering to God.

> Abraham said, My son, God Himself will
> provide a lamb for the burnt offering. So the
> two went on together. (Genesis 22:8)

As we read Romans 4:17, we gain insight into what was on the mind of Abraham as he spoke by faith saying, "God Himself will provide a lamb for the burnt offering." Abraham believed that God would raise Isaac from the dead because Isaac was the miracle child through which Abraham was to become the father of nations. Abraham also understood that the true sacrificial Lamb of God was yet to come into this earth realm. Of course, we now know and understand that the sacrificial Lamb of God was the Incarnate Christ. Let us take a look at a passage from Romans:

> As it is written, I have made you the father of
> many nations. [He was appointed our father]
> in the sight of God in Whom he believed,
> Who gives life to the dead and speaks of the
> non-existent things that [He has foretold
> and promised] as if they [already] existed.
> (Romans 4:17 Amplified Bible).

The message of faith had been preached to Abraham and Abraham chose to believe and confidently trust God.

> And the Scripture, foreseeing that God would
> justify (declare righteous, put in right standing
> with Himself) the Gentiles in consequence
> of faith, proclaimed the Gospel [foretelling
> the glad tidings of a Savior long beforehand]
> to Abraham in the promise, saying, In you
> shall all the nations [of the earth] be blessed.
> (Galatians 3:8 Amplified Bible)

When all physical ability which would allow Abraham and Sarah to manifest the promise of God was totally gone, Abraham looked through the eyes of faith and kept believing God. Faith has see-ability that urges one to create a portal for the release and fulfillment of the divine will of God into the earth realm. According to Romans 4:18, based on the physical condition of Abraham's body, there was no natural reason for him to hope. Physically, there was no reproductive fire in either Abraham or Sarah. Nevertheless, Abraham looked away from the physical and gazed at the spiritual source—his covenant keeping God. That release of faith created a portal for God's miraculous power to be released in Abraham's situation so that the promise of God could be fulfilled.

The Lord Jesus testified that Abraham had eyes of faith and was able to see beyond the physical realm.

> Your forefather Abraham was extremely happy at the hope and prospect of seeing my day (My incarnation); and he did see it and was delighted. (John 8:56 Amplified Bible)

The writer of the Book of Hebrews made a statement about Abraham's ability to see through the eyes of faith so that the Word of Promise could be reflected and realized in the earth:

> So from one man, though he was physically as good as dead, there have sprung descendants whose number is as the stars of heaven and as countless as the innumerable sands of the seashore. These people all died controlled and sustained by their faith, but not having received the tangible fulfillment of [God's] promises, only having seen it and greeted it

from a great distance by faith, and all the while acknowledging and confessing that they were strangers and temporary residents and exiles upon the earth. (Hebrews 11:12-13 Amplified Bible)

Thank God for the redemptive work of Jesus Christ that allows believers to "receive the tangible fulfillment of God's promises." Believers are now in position to partake of what the Old Testament saints longed to see—Redemption.

As a strategic part of redemption, redeemed vessels (believers) are to be led by the Spirit of God. Redeemed vessels are to walk by faith and not by sight. Redeemed vessels do not walk by the dictates of the physical senses, but bring all faculties under the discipline of the Holy Spirit.

So then, brethren, we are debtors, but not to the flesh [we are not obligated to our carnal nature], to live [a life ruled by the standards set up by the dictates] of the flesh. For if you live according to [the dictates of] the flesh, you will surely die. But if through the power of the [Holy] Spirit you are [habitually] putting to death (making extinct, deadening) the [evil] deeds prompted by the body, you shall [really and genuinely] live forever. For all who are led by the Spirit of God are sons of God. (Romans 8:12-14 Amplified Bible)

Believers are no longer debtors to the dictates of sense knowledge, but are free to reflect the image of God in the earth by releasing His ability, His wisdom, and His goodness. Now, since we understand that we are not obligated to obey our flesh, but are free to walk by faith, there are several hindrances to walking by faith that believers need to avoid.

One of the biggest hindrances to the walk of faith is undisciplined affections. In order to avoid the trap of doubting God's power, wisdom, and goodness, believers are not to allow the seen world to regulate their affections. In obedience to Colossians 3:1-2, believers set their affections on things above.

> If then you have been raised with Christ [to a new life, thus sharing His resurrection from the dead], aim at and seek the [rich eternal treasures] that are above, where Christ is, seated at the right hand of God. [Ps. 110:1.] And set your minds and keep them set on what is above (the higher things), not on the things that are on the earth. (Amplified Bible)

Those who walk by faith have crucified the fleshly appetite for lusting after the things of this world. Those who walk by faith continue to steadfastly gaze through the eyes of faith at those things that are eternal and the believer's true reality. Those walking by faith daily put into practice those things faith reveals. Let us take a look at another biblical example of the lives of those walking by faith: Moses.

Moses had all the wealth and prestige one could have, yet after he was aroused by faith and his spiritual eyes were opened, he made a decision that tangible things were worthless compared to what he would gain eternally.

> [Aroused] by faith Moses, when he had grown to maturity and become great, refused to be called the son of Pharaoh's daughter, [Exod. 2:10, 15.] Because he preferred to share the oppression [suffer the hardships] and bear

the shame of the people of God rather than to have the fleeting enjoyment of a sinful life. He considered the contempt and abuse and shame [borne for] the Christ (the Messiah Who was to come) to be greater wealth than all the treasures of Egypt, for he looked forward and away to the reward (recompense). (Hebrews 11:24-26. Amplified Bible)

Another hindrance to avoid is pride. Believers are not to allow pride to dictate their standard of living because pride shuts down the ability to walk by faith. Pride in the heart gives rise to disease in the spiritual eyes making them ineffective to operate in the faith realm. The Church of Laodicea suffered with spiritual eye disease; consequently, they walked in deception rather than faith.

For you say, I am rich; I have prospered and grown wealthy, and I am in need of nothing; and you do not realize and understand that you are wretched, pitiable, poor, blind, and naked. Therefore I counsel you to purchase from Me gold refined and tested by fire, that you may be [truly] wealthy, and white clothes to clothe you and to keep the shame of your nudity from being seen, and salve to put on your eyes, that you may see. (Revelation 3:17-18 Amplified Bible)

Pride in the heart rendered these believers ineffective in reflecting the image of God in the earth.

Although Abraham possessed great material wealth, he did not allow *the pride of life* to infest his eyes of faith. We can assuredly say that Abraham's spiritual eyes were healthy because the Bible declares Abraham was prompted by faith.

> [Prompted] by faith he dwelt as a temporary resident in the land which was designated in the promise [of God, though he was like a stranger] in a strange country, living in tents with Isaac and Jacob, fellow heirs with him of the same promise. [Gen. 12:1-8] For he was [waiting expectantly and confidently] looking forward to the city which has fixed and firm foundations, whose Architect and Builder is God. (Hebrews 11:9-10 Amplified Bible).

The third hindrance to avoid is unstable spiritual character. A lack of Christian character will cause believers to become spiritually blind; consequently, they return to walking by sight rather than faith. The Apostle Peter instructs us to allow Christian character to dwell in us in abundance and as it does, it will keep us from becoming spiritually blind, able to walk (live) only by physical sight.

> For this very reason, adding your diligence [to the divine promises], employ every effort in exercising your faith to develop virtue (excellence, resolution, Christian energy), and to [exercising] virtue [develop] knowledge (intelligence), and in [exercising] knowledge [develop] self-control, and in [exercising] self-control [develop] steadfastness (patience, endurance), and in [exercising] steadfastness [develop] godliness (piety), and in [exercising] godliness [develop] brotherly affection, and in [exercising] brotherly affection [develop]

Christian love. For as these qualities are yours and increasingly abound in you, they will keep [you] from being idle or unfruitful unto the [full personal] knowledge of our Lord Jesus Christ (the Messiah, the Anointed One). For whoever lacks these qualities is blind, [spiritually] shortsighted, seeing only what is near to him, and has become oblivious [to the fact] that he was cleansed from his old sins. (2 Peter 1:5-9 Amplified Bible)

The Apostle Peter states that believers must grow in intimate knowledge of the Lord Jesus Christ beyond their initial encounter with Him at new birth. Believers must move forward into deeply experiencing the qualities that are inherent in Messiah's personality: faith, virtue, knowledge, self-control, patience, godliness, brotherly love, and the God-kind of love. If believers are to stay away from eye disease, these qualities must be in the personality in abundance and not sparingly.

Believers have been blessed by God in order to be a blessing in the earth realm. This condition of *being blessed to be a blessing* is a new creature reality that was given as a covenant promise to Abraham and to his seed.

Now [in Haran] the Lord said to Abram, Go for yourself [for your own advantage] away from your country, from your relatives and your father's house, to the land that I will show you. And I will make of you a great nation, and I will bless you [with abundant increase of favors] and make your name famous and distinguished, and you will be a blessing

43

[dispensing good to others]. (Genesis 12:1-2 Amplified Bible)

In accordance with Second Corinthians 5:17, every individual possessing the nature of Christ is a new creature. The new creature has become an offspring of faithful Abraham; thus, is in position to be a blessing by dispensing good to others.

> For in Christ Jesus you are all sons of God through faith. For as many [of you] as were baptized into Christ [into a spiritual union and communion with Christ, the Anointed One, the Messiah] have put on (clothed yourselves with) Christ. There is [now no distinction] neither Jew nor Greek, there is neither slave nor free, there is not male and female; for you are all one in Christ Jesus. And if you belong to Christ [are in Him Who is Abraham's Seed], then you are Abraham's offspring and [spiritual] heirs according to promise. (Galatians 3:26-29 Amplified Bible).

As new creatures in Christ Jesus, believers have been positioned in God's goodness and anointed with an ability to do good in the earth, even as Jesus did acts of goodness by healing all that were oppressed by the devil.

> How God anointed and consecrated Jesus of Nazareth with the [Holy] Spirit and with strength and ability and power; how He went about doing good and, in particular, curing all who were harassed and oppressed by [the

power of] the devil, for God was with Him.
(Acts 10:38 Amplified Bible).

As new creatures in Christ, we are to imitate Christ and
continue *His work of faith* in the earth realm. The anointing
to heal and deliver was made available to us by the power of
the Holy Spirit. To flow in the anointing, we must believe in
the redemptive work of Jesus and walk by faith. The Bible
declares that attesting signs will follow those who believe in
the Lord Jesus Christ:

> And these attesting signs will accompany
> those who believe; in My name they will drive
> out demons; they will speak in new languages;
> They will pick up serpents; and [even] if they
> drink anything deadly, it will not hurt them;
> they will lay their hands on the sick, and they
> will get well. (Mark 16:17-18 Amplified Bible)

Faith through grace has placed believers in a position of
power and honor, giving each the ability to reflect God's image
in the earth: His nature, His ability, His goodness. In reference
to the phrase, "position of power and honor," the Spirit of
Glory is at work in the lives of believers removing whatever
would hinder them from fulfilling God's original mandate.
The name, *Spirit of Glory*, is a reference to that facet of the
Holy Spirit's ministry employed in restoring those who come
to the Lord in faith to a position of honor: the God appointed
place in creation where a manifestation of the nature of God
can be experienced and reflected in the earth. The Apostle
Paul declared:

> Moreover whom he did predestinate, them he
> also called: and whom he called, them he also

justified: and whom he justified, them he also
glorified." (Romans 8:30)

Thus, as a blood-bought right of glorification, the justified
are in a position of power and honor which makes it legally
possible for them to walk by faith and not by sight, to minister
in both the spiritual and earthly realms.

The anointing that was on Christ, as He reflected the
Father's image in the earth, is also on believers today. As
a part of God's glorification process, believers have been
predestinated and anointed to release God's goodness in
the earth realm. As new creatures in Christ, possessing the
ability to reflect God's image of goodness to those in need of
experiencing His presence, let us make every effort to move
away from whatever would hinder us from walking by faith.

## CHAPTER FIVE

# DIVINE WISDOM

From the previous chapter, we learned that an intricate part of the ability to reflect God's image in the earth was the willingness to trust in God's wisdom and allow His wisdom to become our vocabulary and lifestyle. In view of this truth, let us start this chapter by defining the word *wisdom*.

A general definition of the word, *wisdom,* is the ability to rightly apply acquired knowledge. We collect all types of knowledge through the use of our five senses and the faculty of the intellect. This collection of knowledge makes its way into the heart (one's personality) for storage and distribution. Although there are many external resources for acquiring knowledge, there are only two types of applications employed: worldly or godly wisdom. Let us take a look at the difference between the two applications:

- Worldly wisdom may be viewed as the application of acquired knowledge that is based on human opinions, cultural and traditional mandates, or demonic influences. According to First John 2:16, there are basically three things that characterize worldly wisdom: the lust of the eyes, the lust of the flesh, and the pride of life. Worldly wisdom establishes its own standards of right and wrong, and can adamantly stand opposed to God's standard.

- Godly wisdom is the counsel of God—what God is saying to do about situations of life. Therefore, God is the source of godly wisdom. Godly wisdom always establishes the righteous standard of God in the life. The beauty of godly wisdom is its accessibility to anyone who is humble enough to recognize the need for it. The Apostle James states, "If you need wisdom— if you want to know what God wants you to do—ask him, and he will gladly tell you. He will not resent you asking. But when you ask him, be sure that you really expect him to answer, for a doubtful mind is as unsettled as a wave of the sea that is driven and tossed by the wind." (James 1:5-7 NLT)

God expects believers to trust in and confidently rely on godly wisdom and lean not to human understanding of how to rightly apply knowledge obtained. Proverbs 3:5-6 states, "trust in the LORD with all thine heart; and lean not unto thine own understanding. In all thine ways acknowledge him, and he shall direct thy paths." In this verse, we have God's promise that if we would not rely on human reasoning for the right application of knowledge obtained, God Himself would direct the path of our decision-making: when and what we should do about situations in life.

Before King Solomon's heart was corrupted by idolatry, he freely flowed in the wisdom of God. As we study the events in King Solomon's life, the Bible attests to the fact that God gave Solomon an unprecedented degree of wisdom.

> In that night did God appear unto Solomon, and said unto him, Ask what I shall give thee. And Solomon said unto God, Thou hast shewed

great mercy unto David my father, and hast made me to reign in his stead. Now, O LORD, God, let thy promise unto David my father be established: for thou hast made me king over a people like the dust of the earth in multitude. Give me now wisdom and knowledge, that I may go out and come in before this people: for who can judge this thy people, that is so great? And God said Solomon, Because this was in thine heart, and thou hast not asked riches, wealth, or honour, nor the life of thine enemies, neither yet has asked long life; but hast asked wisdom and knowledge for thyself, that thou mayest judge my people, over whom I have made thee king: Wisdom and knowledge is granted unto thee; and I will give thee riches, and wealth, and honour, such as none of the kings have had that have been before thee, neither shall there any after thee have the like. (2 Chronicles 1:11-12)

Unfortunately, we also see that King Solomon did not always operate in the godly wisdom graced upon his life. When King Solomon stopped relying on God's wisdom and took the counsel of his ungodly wives, the voice of godly wisdom no longer had a place in King Solomon's ear, and his heart strayed from pure affection toward God. In short, when Solomon stopped trusting in godly wisdom, his heart became divided in loyalty toward God.

The LORD had clearly instructed his people not to intermarry with those nations, because the women they married would lead them to worship their gods. Yet Solomon insisted on loving them anyway. He had seven hundred wives and three hundred concubines. And sure enough, they led his heart away from the LORD. In Solomon's old age, they turned his heart to worship their gods instead of trusting only in the LORD his God, as his father, David, had done. (1 Kings 11:2-5 NLT)

Let Solomon's ending be a warning to every believer not to stray from obedience to God's commands, but passionately lend the heart to desire the counsel of God.

When godly wisdom is applied, it will protect believers from wrong decisions and keep the heart pure before God. The Book of Proverbs confirms this truth: "Pay attention to my wisdom, listen carefully to my wise counsel. Then you will learn to be discreet and will store up knowledge." (5:1-2 NLT) Godly wisdom is always available to anyone who has an ear to hear and a heart to obey its counsel.

There are several passages in the Old Testament which illustrate how victorious mankind becomes when there is a willingness to hear and obey the wisdom of God.

◆ After obeying the counsel of God, Jacob, while working for his uncle Laban, was victorious in spite of all Laban's plotting for his failure (Genesis 30:31-43; 31:10-11). Wisdom taught Jacob that failure was not his portion.

◆ Obedience to the counsel of God caused Gideon to triumph over an army much larger than his small 300-man army (Judges Chapter eight).

◆ Queen Esther received and obeyed the counsel of God and saved her people from total annihilation (Esther chapters 4, 5 and 7).

◆ David, after the disaster of Ziglag, obeyed the counsel of God and regained all that he had lost and more besides that which belonged to him (1Samuel Chapter 30).

God's counsel was deemed a vital necessity of life to each of these Old Testament individuals. Each of these individuals operated in faith which came as a result of obeying the counsel of God. In our generation, we have majored so much on getting our way and rubber stamping our way as being God's way that our quality of faith is weak and in some believers, it is inactive. Remember our working definition of faith is *"the leaning of the entire human personality on God in absolute trust in God's ability, wisdom, and power."* Consequently, the evidence that faith in God's wisdom is active is our obedience to His counsel.

The written Word of God is an unfailing source for acquiring beneficial knowledge. The knowledge we receive from the proper study of the Word of God is called revelatory knowledge because its meaning is revealed to us by the power of the Holy Spirit. In addition to being a source for acquiring beneficial knowledge, the Bible is an unending source of wisdom. However, in order to allow this unending source to influence our lives, we must be mindful of our approach to the written Word. What does that statement mean? Simply this: We say that God wants us to study the written Word so that He may direct our lives, yet we purposefully read the written Word in order to pull verses to support selfish desires and then through human efforts, we try to bring those desires to pass. When these efforts are not fruitful, some believers blame God for the failure and become very angry with Him. In order to avoid these "hit and miss" applications, let us pursue an inspired understanding of how to rightly apply the principles in the written Word rather than using the Word of God to support selfish desires.

To acquire an inspired understanding of the right application of the written Word one will need to engage in Spirit-led study rather than leaning to one's own understanding of how the principles of the Kingdom of God operate. Entering into Spirit-led study of the Word of God will require three things: (1) confidently trusting that God is the source of the wisdom needful, (2) humility of heart to discard previously conceived faulty concepts, and (3) a willingness to hear and obey God's counsel.

When godly wisdom is applied to any given situation, the holy character of God is evidenced. In the Holy Spirit's work of guiding believers by godly wisdom, He will never go outside of the holy character of the Godhead. If our application of the written Word is not in alignment with God's holy nature, its origin is not God. Now, let us take a look at the character of godly wisdom and give the Holy Spirit an opportunity to breathe upon our understanding of the direction He guides believers. The Epistles are a marvelous place to obtain insight into the character of godly wisdom.

Colossians 2:3-4, 6-7 tells us where to find wisdom and admonishes us to continue steadfastly in that source. Jesus is our source of godly wisdom; thus, it becomes imperative that we regulate our lives and conduct ourselves in union with Him. Regulating our lives in union with Christ is an eternal truth that the Holy Spirit will not violate, regardless of our situation in life.

> IN HIM all the treasures of [divine] wisdom (comprehensive insight into the ways and purposes of God) and [all the riches of spiritual knowledge and enlightenment are stored up

and lie hidden. I say this in order that no one may mislead and delude you by plausible and persuasive and attractive arguments and beguiling speech...As you have therefore received Christ, [even] Jesus the Lord, [so] walk (regulate your lives and conduct yourselves) in union with and conformity to Him. Have the roots [of your being] firmly and deeply planted [in Him, fixed and founded in Him], being continually built up in Him, becoming increasingly more confirmed and established in the faith, just as you were taught, and abounding and overflowing in it with thanksgiving. (Amplified Bible)

There are several instructions in these verses that we need to consider:

→ There are two sources of wisdom flowing, but only one of those sources brings godly wisdom that will not leave us in delusion as to what is the truth. The stand that believers are to take is to seek wisdom from in Him, the Lord Jesus Christ, and not be misled by arguments that are persuasive and attractive, but delusive in content.

→ The wisdom which comes from Jesus Christ will give us *"comprehensive insight into the ways and purposes of God."* The Words which Christ speaks are full of life and ability, enlightening and refreshing the soul. We are to learn from Him and imitate His character and this we will do when we listen to obey His wisdom. As we yield to the guidance of the Holy Spirit, He will make Jesus a reality in our souls (John 14:26; 16:13).

➔ We are to regulate our lives by the wisdom we have learned from Christ Jesus. Godly wisdom is imparted to us so that we might experience freedom in Christ. Do more than hear what Christ has to say—put His instructions to work in the life. As we conduct our lives in consistency with His wisdom, our souls are transformed more and more into His character.

➔ Do not allow the affections of the heart to become divided in loyalty to Jesus because divided affections damage the believer's root system. In the natural, roots are very vital to the healthy growth of living things. Roots spread themselves out to anchor the plant and search for the resources needful to satisfy the plant's hunger, thus, assuring healthy growth. In a similar way, the affections are the believer's root system. Their function is to supply support and nourishment to the soul. As the soul longs, the affections seek the resources needful to satisfy those longings. Sinful desire causes the affections to look for pleasures which violate God's intended function for an individual's faculties. In order for our affections to function as God created them to function, the desires of the heart are to be firmly established in Jesus Christ. An attitude of thanksgiving is one method which will help believers' roots (affections) remain established in Christ. A thankful heart cultivates loyalty in the affections and keeps believers from having a divided heart which fluctuates between complaining and faultfinding.

First Corinthians 1:30 through 2:15 states that we are in Christ and He is our wisdom, righteousness, sanctification, and redemption. Let us take a look at several of these verses from the Amplified Bible:

> But it is from Him that you have your life in Christ Jesus, Whom God made our Wisdom from God, [revealed to us a knowledge of the divine plan of salvation previously hidden, manifesting itself as] our Righteousness [thus making us upright and putting us in right standing with God], and our Consecration [making us pure and holy], and our Redemption [providing our ransom from eternal penalty for sin]. So then, as it is written, Let him who boasts and proudly rejoices and glories, boast and proudly rejoice and glory in the Lord. (1 Corinthians 1:30-31 Amplified Bible)

Since Christ is all to us, our boasting and rejoicing is in His ability that flows through us. When it comes to decisions of the conscience or doctrines to live by, we do not operate in worldly wisdom, but in the wisdom we receive from Christ Jesus. Our goal is to give to others the wisdom which comes from Christ, so that their faith will rest on a sure foundation. The Holy Spirit will guide believers into the wisdom which is in Christ Jesus—the Living Word.

> As for myself, brethren, when I came to you, I did not come proclaiming to you the testimony and evidence or mystery and secret of God [concerning what He has done through Christ for the salvation of men] in lofty words of eloquence or human philosophy and wisdom; For I resolved to know nothing (to be acquainted with nothing, to make a display of the knowledge of nothing, and to be conscious of nothing) among you except Jesus Christ (the Messiah) and Him crucified. And I was

in (passed into a state of) weakness and fear (dread) and great trembling [after I had come] among you. And my language and my message were not set forth in persuasive (enticing and plausible) words of wisdom, but they were in demonstration of the [Holy] Spirit and power [a proof by the Spirit and power of God, operating on me and stirring in the minds of my hearers the most holy emotions and thus persuading them], So that your faith might not rest in the wisdom of men (human philosophy), but in the power of God. (1 Corinthians 2:1-5 Amplified Bible)

Now, notice that the Apostle Paul states that there are two types of wisdom in the world: human and divine. As we speak to men concerning salvation, we must choose to stay away from human wisdom and operate in divine wisdom—and that with fear and trembling.

Pride in the soul causes individuals to flaunt earthly knowledge (ungodly wisdom). Paul refers to earthly wisdom as "*lofty words of eloquence or human philosophy and wisdom.*" There are those who will use "lofty words" and "human philosophy" to twist the Word of God in order to support their agendas. We must continue to guard our hearts from the spirit of error that is in the world, as Jesus did in the wilderness temptation.

In another place, the Apostle Paul refers to ungodly wisdom as "*cunning craftiness lying in wait to deceive*" *(Ephesians 4:14).* The way to avoid becoming a prey to false teaching is to speak the truth while walking in the love of God (Ephesians 4:15). We are to always desire truth in the inward part and minister from the anointing which comes from the wisdom of the Spirit of Truth. We are to reflect godly wisdom in the earth realm—not human philosophy, cultural superstitions, or traditions which keep us from experiencing the power in the Word of God.

Since Christ is our wisdom, the task at hand is for believers to move away from anything that might bring a blemish to the Cross of Christ.

> Therefore, my dear ones, as you have always obeyed [my suggestions], so now, not only [with the enthusiasm you would show] in my presence but much more because I am absent, work out (cultivate, carry out to the goal, and fully complete) your own salvation with reverence and awe and trembling (self-distrust, with serious caution, tenderness of conscience, watchfulness against temptation, timidly shrinking from whatever might offend God and discredit the name of Christ). [Not in your own strength] for it is God Who is all the while effectually at work in you [energizing and creating in you the power and desire], both to will and to work for His good pleasure and satisfaction and delight. (Philippians 2:12-13 Amplified Bible)

There are several very helpful instructions in this passage:

➔ We are advised that obedience to the truth should operate in us regardless of who is present. We must be mindful that once God has placed someone in our lives to disciple us with inspired truth, we are to remain steadfast to the teachings they impart and not be persuaded that the truth they imparted is a lie. The Scripture warns us that in the last days, false teachers will arise and change the truth into a lie in order to gratify human flesh (Second Timothy 4:3-4). Know and understand this principle: pride in the heart brings forth deception on the lips.

→ We are instructed that deliverance from worldly thinking is a work of faith which must be cultivated, carried out to the goal, and fully completed in the prescribed manner: with reverence, awe, and trembling.

→ We are to put no confidence in flesh ability to produce anything which is Kingdom productive. We are to engage in self-distrust and that with serious caution, tenderness of conscience, and watchfulness against temptation.

→ Believers are to move away from teachings (doctrines) that will offend God and/or discredit the name of Christ. Regardless of how good it might sound, if it is not inspired by the Holy Spirit, it is not Kingdom productive. If what we are teaching did not come by the wisdom of God, it is not usable in the Kingdom of God, and should not depart from our lips as food for the children of God.

→ Only by the grace of God will we be able to produce anything in our souls that is useful to reflect the image of God in the earth, thus we must not take pride in flesh abilities, but hunger and thirst after God's right way of thinking and doing. We are to completely desire to be a trophy of God's wisdom and grace.

How does one identify God's wisdom in order to guard the heart against anything which is not? Good question! In James 3:13-18, we are told how to differentiate between the two types of wisdom that are in the earth realm.

Who is there among you who is wise and intelligent? Then let him by his noble living show forth his [good] works with the [unobtrusive] humility [which is the proper attribute] of true wisdom. But if you have bitter jealousy (envy) and contention (rivalry, self-ambition) in your hearts, do not pride yourselves on it and thus be in defiance of and false to the Truth. This [superficial] wisdom is not such as comes down from above, but is earthly, unspiritual (animal), even devilish (demoniacal). For wherever there is jealousy (envy) and contention (rivalry and selfish ambition), there will also be confusion (unrest, disharmony, rebellion) and all sorts of evil and vile practices. But the wisdom from above is first of all pure (undefiled); then it is peace-loving, courteous (considerate, gentle). [It is willing to] yield to reason, full of compassion and good fruits; it is wholehearted and straightforward, impartial and unfeigned (free from doubts, wavering, and insincerity). And the harvest of righteousness (of conformity to God's will in thought and deed) is [the fruit of the seed] sown in peace by those who work for and make peace [in themselves and in others, that peace which means concord, agreement, and harmony between individuals, with undisturbedness, in a peaceful mind free from fears and agitating passions and moral conflicts]. (Amplified Bible)

The Apostle James tells us that the *proper attire* of godly wisdom is humility (a sober estimation of one's strength and weaknesses) which is unobtrusive (not blatant, or aggressive, pushy, showy or impertinent)[2] Now, understand that the first stop in operating in godly wisdom is to have a sober estimation of one's abilities and to understand that without God's ability and wisdom there will be a shortage in the power needful to deliver anyone from bondage. Again, the evidence that we are not operating in godly wisdom is obtrusive behavior which is blatantly aggressive, pushy, showy, and undesirably noticeable.

The characteristics of ungodly wisdom consist of jealousy (envy) and contention (rivalry, selfish ambition) in the heart. These are the characteristics that cause the heart to be in defiance to the truth. If one is to operate in godly wisdom, the heart has to be purged of jealousy and contention. According to James, if we allow jealousy and contention to remain in the heart, the heart will experience unrest and become a dwelling place for every sort of evil practice. This warning against spiritual digression should incite us to walk in the wisdom of God rather than operate in sensual earthly wisdom. James describes superficial wisdom as earthly, unspiritual (coming from the lower nature of an individual: animal), even devilish (demoniacal in origin). For this reason, all types of evil and vile practices find their home in superficial wisdom. Operating in superficial wisdom is a life of digressing from the freedom the new creature is to experience and reflect in the earth realm. Once again, understand that walking in anything other than the wisdom of God as the standard of living will cause a digression in the life of a believer. However, when believers operate in the wisdom of God, it keeps the spiritual life moving forward in God's divine purposes.

The wisdom that comes from God can plainly be identified by its attributes which depict the very nature of God:

---

[2] Webster's Seventh New Collegiate Dictionary

◆ Pure speaks to us of being undefiled by the philosophy of humans, the cultural norms of society, or the prejudices of one's own heart. Divine wisdom is holy— it conforms in all ways to the character of God.

◆ Peace-loving is the increase which comes from allowing the fruit of peace to influence the heart. Godly wisdom flows through the fruit of peace; therefore, does not disturb our minds, but settles the mind so that there are no fears, agitating passions, or moral conflicts bargaining in the soul. The result of operating in godly wisdom is a harvest of righteousness, defined as conformity to God's will in thought and deed. If the counsel we offer others does not conform to God's will in thought and deed, it is not godly wisdom and will not produce in the recipient a harvest of righteousness. The increase which comes from operating in the wisdom of God is concord, agreement, and harmony to the will of God. When we operate in the wisdom of God for any given circumstance, peace is present and it will eject worry and hostility from the soul.

◆ Courteous means that godly wisdom is not pushy or rude, but considerate of other's character development. Godly wisdom respects the personage of others and is considerate of them: the course they take in life. Godly wisdom takes the time to listen to others, and the Holy Spirit, in order to give right counsel. Those operating and imparting godly wisdom are gentle, not hard or unteachable. Those operating in godly wisdom do not insist on having their own way. Individuals operating in godly wisdom are easily corrected and persuaded to follow whatever direction God would have them to pursue.

◆ Compassionate speaks of godly wisdom containing a deep desire to see others made whole and releasing the ability to bring wholeness into the lives of others. Godly wisdom is not moved by the wantonness of the lives of others, but motivated by the love of God to speak a revelation from God that will bring transformation into the life.

◆ Wholehearted and straightforward speaks to us of being undivided in loyalty or allegiance to an individual for the purpose of giving them counsel which will positively influence their lives. Godly wisdom shows no partiality, but is quite impartial in counsel. There are no selfish desires in godly wisdom. There is no apathy or misguided empathy in godly wisdom. The wisdom which comes from God is not deceptive or crocked in its application or speech: what it says to one it says to all. In godly wisdom, there is a straightforwardness that will not cause one to stumble or grope in darkness.

◆ Unfeigned (free from doubts, wavering and insincerity) depicts the verity and dependability of godly wisdom. Godly wisdom is genuine and has no hypocrisy in it. Godly wisdom doesn't measure its deliverance of truth by natural blood relationships, but dispenses to all the portions needful for transformation in the life. Godly wisdom passionately pursues the release of God's goodness in the life of the hearer.

Earthly (superficial) wisdom finds a place in the life of a believer through pride which is operating in the heart. Pride in the heart sets itself up as a god, bringing with it its own standard of morals. Walking in the fear of the Lord is really the solution which the God-kind of wisdom will employ. The Bible describes *the fear of the Lord* as the attitude of heart which has a reverential honor and respect for God. Those walking in the fear of the Lord move away from evil and steadfastly cleave to righteousness. According to Psalm 111:10, it is through the fear of the Lord that the human heart is positioned to hear and obey the wisdom of God.

The reverent fear and worship of the Lord is the beginning of Wisdom and skill [the preceding and the first essential, the prerequisite and the alphabet]; a good understanding, wisdom, and meaning have all those who do [the will of the Lord]. Their praise of Him endures forever. (Psalm 111:10 Amplified Bible)

Since the fear of the Lord is the beginning of receiving divine wisdom, only those entertaining foolishness in their hearts will turn away from it.

The reverent and worshipful fear of the Lord is the beginning and the principal and choice part of knowledge [its starting point and its essence]; but fools despise skillful and godly Wisdom, instruction, and discipline. (Proverbs 1:7 Amplified Bible)

Because mankind was created with free will, we must choose which type of wisdom we will allow to govern our lives. The advice which comes to us from the Apostles Paul and James is to reflect God's image in the earth by choosing to walk in godly wisdom.

## CHAPTER SIX

# SONSHIP

As we approach the study of sonship, let us first agree that the emphasis of the word *sonship* is not gender, but a reference to the new position believers (male and female) have in Christ Jesus. Basically, there are two phrases used to describe the adoptive element of sonship: children of God and sons of God. The phrases *children of God* and *sons of God* speak to us of having the very nature of God in the believer's recreated human spirit; thus, the emphasis of these two phrases is on individuals becoming offspring of God and heirs in the Kingdom of God.

In the New Testament, there are several passages which use the same Greek word to describe both phrases. For example, John 1:12 states, "But as many as received him, to them gave he power to become the sons of God, even to them that believe on his name." From the Greek, the word used for "sons" is *tĕknŏn* which means *a child (as produced)—child, daughter, son.*[3] The emphasis of the phrase, "sons of God," is on becoming a part of God's family through faith in Jesus Christ. The same Greek word is used in Romans 8:16, 17 and 21 in the phrase *"children of God".*

---

[3] Strong's Exhaustive Concordance, #5043

> The Spirit itself beareth witness with our spirit, that we are the children of God. And if children, then heirs; heirs of God, and joint-heirs with Christ; if so be that we suffer with him, that we may be also glorified together... Because the creature itself also shall be delivered from the bondage of corruption into the glorious liberty of the children of God.

As a side note about this passage, using the word, *itself*, as a reference to the Holy Spirit is incorrect. The Holy Spirit is not an "it," but the third person of the Godhead and should be referred to as such.

Just as the full scope of salvation has a past, present, and future unfolding, these verses in Romans brings into view the eschatological component of adoption. There is a futuristic glorious freedom determined by God for the *"now"* children of God which creation is groaning to experience. Thus, these verses should not be used to support the erroneous belief that believers *"will become"* children of God at some future date. Let us take a look at John's testimony about the present and futuristic components of adoption.

> See what [an incredible] quality of love the Father has given (shown, bestowed on) us, that we should [be permitted to] be named and called and counted the children of God! And so we are! The reason that the world does not know (recognize, acknowledge) us is that it does not know (recognize, acknowledge) Him. Beloved, we are [even here and] now God's children; it is not yet disclosed (made clear) what we shall be [hereafter], but we know that when He comes and is manifested, we shall [as

God's children] resemble and be like Him, for we shall see Him just as He [really] is. (1 John 3:1-2 Amplified Bible).

From this passage, we understand that believers are presently God's children and are engaged in a progressive unfolding glorification process in which more and more of the character of Christ is being formed in the soul during their stay on the earth. Although this glorification progression is currently taking place, there is yet a future glory which God has predestined for believers to experience at the appearance of Christ. When Christ appears, the manifestation of the promised futuristic glory will occur and believers will be like Him—possessing a glorified body. This promise comes into view in Paul's statement: "And having chosen them, he called them to come to him. And he gave them right standing with himself, and he promised them his glory." (Romans 8:3 NLT)

In reference to the Body of Christ, which consists of both male and female, the emphasis of sonship is not gender, but position of oneness in the household of faith. From the Greek definition of the word, t🔲knŏn, both male and female believers bear the positional title "sons of God" just as both are "children of God". Paul informed the Galatians that in Christ Jesus there is no distinction—all are one in Christ Jesus.

> For in Christ Jesus you are all sons of God through faith. For as many [of you] as were baptized into Christ [into a spiritual union and communion with Christ, the Anointed One, the Messiah] have put on (clothed yourselves with) Christ. There is [now no distinction] neither Jew nor Greek, there is neither slave nor free, there is not male and female; for you are all one

in Christ Jesus. (Galatians 3:26-28 Amplified Bible)

We must also note that the Greek word used in this passage for "sons" is *huiŏs* meaning *child, son*[4] and refers more to level of maturity than gender. Now, let us keep in mind that where God makes no distinction, let us not make one, but rather move swiftly to apply His wisdom as we fellowship with other believers in the Body of Christ.

Once again, *sonship* is the believer's (male and female) legal position in the Kingdom of God. The Apostle Paul used the term in several epistles to describe the new relationship believers have with God. Although Paul's probable use of the Roman system of adoption for a backdrop is highly debated among theologians; nevertheless, the honor placed on adoption by Roman law is quite helpful in understanding the adoption of believers.

In the Roman world of the first century, an adopted individual was deliberately chosen (often as an adult) to perpetuate the new parent's name and become an heir of the estate. Roman society considered the adopted individual equal with one of natural birth; therefore, an adopted individual had the same rights and privileges as one naturally born into a family. The Greek word Paul used to explain the believer's new position is *huiŏthĕsia* meaning *"the placing as a son, i.e., adoption"*.[5]

One of the beautiful aspects of sonship is that the adoption of believers was not an afterthought in the mind of God, but was fully planned by God from eternity—God predestined us to be adopted through the redemptive work of Jesus Christ. The adoption of believers is not the results of human merit,

[4] Strong's Exhaustive Concordance, #5207
[5] Ibid., #5206

but entirely an expression of the Father's work of love and grace through Christ Jesus.

In Ephesians chapter one, Paul explains that God, as a loving Father, predestinated us to be adopted as His very own children so that we might be holy, blameless, and loved. In other words, it pleased the Father to choose us to become His very own *adopted* children—it was His good pleasure!

> Blessed be the God and Father of our Lord Jesus Christ, who hath blessed us with all spiritual blessings in heavenly places in Christ: According as he hath chosen us in him before the foundation of the world, that we should be holy and without blame before him in love: Having predestinated us unto the adoption of children by Jesus Christ to himself, according to the good pleasure of his will, to the praise of the glory of his grace, wherein he hath made us accepted in the beloved. (Ephesians 1:3-6)

The Amplified Bible states that "He chose us [actually picked us out for Himself as His own] in Christ before the foundation of the world..." (Ephesians 1:4). Now, that's good news!

Because Adam was God's son (Luke 3:38), his fall in the Garden of Eden caused mankind to become alienated from their Creator and Father. Before adoption, we were orphans, destitute, and alienated from God, but now, through faith in the redemptive work of Christ Jesus, believers have been accepted into God's family as His very own children. Not only are we redeemed and forgiven, we are children of God. Alienation has been removed! In addition, our adoption into the family of God has caused our eternal position to shift and realign with God's original blueprint for mankind—one of dominion and authority through sonship. Through adoption, we are children of God, bearing His very nature on the inside of us. The Apostle Paul describes this new nature as the *righteousness of God* in Christ Jesus.

> For he hath made him to be sin for us, who knew no sin; that we might be made the righteousness of God in him. (2 Corinthians 5:21)

Believers stand before the Father as *"consecrated and blameless"* redeemed vessels of honor, with the legal right to reflect His image in the earth realm.

In sonship, the spiritual condition of believers changed from purposeless to purposeful. Adoption has given believers a new position in life. In this new position, believers have the legal right and honor of perpetuating the name of their new parent and the values that name represents. As a matter of fact, in the natural, the adopter chose the individual for that very purpose: to gain an heir who would perpetuate the family's name and values. With an heir in place, the name and value system of the adopter would be continuously reflected in the earth.

It is God's desire to have His image continuously reflected in the earth through those created in His image and after His likeness. Adoption made the fulfillment of this desire possible. As the adopted children of God, believers have a legal right and the glorious honor of perpetuating the Father's name, as well as the values of the Kingdom of God, in the earth.

Jesus stands as the believer's example of and blueprint for perpetuating the Father's name and the value system of the Kingdom in the earth. What did Jesus do? In the Book of Acts,

Luke tells us that Jesus went about *"doing good and destroying the works of the devil."*

> How God anointed Jesus of Nazareth with the Holy Ghost and with power: who went about doing good, and healing all that were oppressed of the devil; for God was with Him, and we are witnesses of all things which he did both in the land of the Jews, and in Jerusalem. (Acts 10:38-39a)

From this passage, the will of the Father and His kingdom values are plainly displayed; that is, the Father wants mankind to experience wholeness and freedom from all demonic oppression. God anointed Jesus with the Holy Spirit and power for the purpose of spreading goodwill in the earth and delivering people from the ill will of the devil. Always remember that the true image of God is goodwill: He is the God of goodwill toward men (Luke 2:14). Jesus received an anointing of power, equipping Him to reflect the goodwill of the Father in the earth.

Our second witness to the acts of Jesus comes from the "beloved" Apostle John. John tells us that Jesus was manifested to destroy the works of the devil.

> He that committeth sin is of the devil; for the devil sinneth from the beginning. For this purpose the Son of God was manifested, that he might destroy the works of the devil. (1 John 3:8)

Once again, the works Jesus did testify to the will of the Father and reflect the true image of the Father. The Father is not putting sickness on mankind to teach them something.

The Father wants to take sickness away from our midst and deliver mankind from all the works of the devil—for this purpose was the Son of God manifested. For this purpose are the *adopted* sons of God commissioned to exercise dominion in the earth realm. This brings us to our third witness. Our third witness comes from the Book of Matthew. Several verses in Matthew chapter ten testify that preaching and healing are the evidence that the Kingdom of heaven is at hand and the will of the Father is being accomplished.

> These twelve Jesus sent forth, and commanded them, saying, Go not into the way of the Gentiles, and into any city of the Samaritans enter ye not: but go rather to the lost sheep of the house of Israel. And as ye go, preach, saying, The Kingdom of heaven is at hand. Heal the sick, cleanse the lepers, raise the dead, cast out devils: freely ye have received, freely give. (Matthew 10:5-8)

Now, notice that Jesus is giving the disciples the opportunity to put into practice the things they have observed in His ministry. His actions can be likened to the big brother of the house teaching the younger children of the house how to represent the family in public. Let us take a look at another passage from the Book of Matthew.

> Go then and make disciples of all the nations, baptizing them into the name of the Father and of the Son and of the Holy Spirit. Teaching them to observe everything that I have commanded you, and behold, I am with you all the days (perpetually, uniformly, and on every occasion), to the [very] close and

consummation of the age. Amen (so let it be). (Matthew 28:19-20 Amplified Bible)

This passage is referred to as the Great Commission of the Church. The statement, *"teaching them to observe everything that I have commanded you,"* commissioned believers to perpetuate the family values and the name of the Father because these are the things which Jesus taught during His earthly ministry. Jesus taught the disciples to cast out demons and heal the sick. As Jesus did the will of the Father, many were introduced to the Kingdom of God. Once again, Jesus is our example of perpetuating the name of the Father and the values of the Kingdom of God in the earth realm. Jesus is our example of how to reflect the image of God in the earth.

## CHAPTER SEVEN

# SONSHIP AND THE DOMINION MANDATE

L et us take a moment to lay a firm foundation for why
sonship is the legal way for operating in the dominion
mandate. In accordance with Genesis 1:26, God gave the right
to operate in power and authority in the earth realm to those
created in His image.

> God said, Let Us [Father, Son, and Holy Spirit]
> make mankind in Our image, after Our
> likeness, and let them have complete authority
> over the fish of the sea, the birds of the air,
> the [tame] beasts, and over all of the earth,
> over everything that creeps upon the earth.
> (Genesis 1:26 Amplified Bible)

Adam, as God's son, operated in this dominion mandate
until the fall into disobedience. However, since the crucifixion
and resurrection of Jesus Christ (the last Adam), those
expressing faith in Jesus' redemptive work become sons of
God and are restored to God's original mandate. As sons of
God, *recreated* in the image of God, believers have the capacity
to operate in God's original mandate for mankind. Thus

sonship became the legal position for mankind to once again operate in power and authority in the earth realm. What the first Adam lost, Jesus, as the last Adam, regained.

> For just as [because of their union of nature] in Adam all people die, so also [by virtue of their union of nature] shall all in Christ be made alive...Thus it is written, The first man Adam became a living being (an individual personality); the last Adam (Christ) became a life-giving Spirit [restoring the dead to life]. (1 Corinthians 15:22, 45 Amplified Bible)

Although sonship is now the legal position for the exercise of dominion in the earth, that legal position is not without opposition, especially when believers operate in faulty images of God. One opposition which stands in the way of some believers exercising dominion in the earth is the belief that evil is a sovereign mysterious act of God. Without the correct image of the character of God, it will be difficult, if not impossible, to fulfill the dominion mandate. For this reason, it is vital that believers obtain the truth concerning the character of God. Studying the Word of God, coupled with the sweet communion of the Holy Spirit, will assist with aligning the thoughts of believers with the true image of *who* God is and *what* God allows.

The Genesis' mandate consisted of both kingly and priestly authority. Now, let us turn aside and take a look at each of these components. In priestly authority, supplication is made on behalf of others and self in alignment with the Father's will. The duties believers are expected to employ under the priestly anointing are: praying for others (including your enemies), repairing the breach, and teaching Kingdom principles.

Jesus' earthly ministry serves as our example of how to reflect God's image in the earth through priestly authority. Jesus often arose early to find a place of solitude where He could pray to the Father (Luke 6:12, 9:28). John chapter seventeen records the Lord's supplication for the apostles and all who would believe upon His name. The Lord engaged in intense supplication in the Garden of Gethsemane (Mark 14:32). The Book of Hebrews records His moments of supplication as one with "strong crying and tears to Him Who was [always] able to save Him [out] from death," (5:7 Amplified Bible). From the cross, we see Jesus, once again, engaged in supplication for mankind as He prayed, "Father forgive them for they know not what they do," (Luke 23:34).

In addition to offering supplication and petitions, those in priestly ministry were to teach the people the commands of God. The Bible records that Jesus went from place to place "preaching and teaching" the people about the Kingdom of God (Luke 8:1); He also sent the twelve disciples to do the same (Luke 9:6).

In kingly authority, one is expected to decree the name of Jesus and the Kingdom's standard of righteousness in the earth, always aligning the decrees with the Father's will. Once again, it is through the public ministry of Jesus Christ that we gain insight into walking in kingly authority in the earth realm. From the beginning to the end of Jesus' public ministry, He was engaged in establishing the Father's will in the earth realm. Although Jesus is God the Son, by Sovereign design and for our benefit, He did no works until He received an anointing from the Holy Spirit to administer and to establish the Kingdom of God in the earth. Jesus continuously demonstrated Kingdom authority by perpetuating the family's values and the name of the Father in the earth through signs and wonders. Demons recognized His authority (Matthew 8:28-29) and people acknowledge Him as the Son of David (covenant mankind) with authority to establish the Kingdom of God in the earth (Mark 10:46-48).

As the sons of God observe to do the teachings of the Son of God, we, too, will effectively reflect the image of God in this earth realm.

## CHAPTER EIGHT

# THE LANGUAGE OF ADOPTION

When Jesus explained the dynamics of citizenship in the Kingdom of God to the first disciples, He spoke the language of adoption. The language of adoption always echoes the Father's goodwill for the lives of His children. Let's take a look at a passage from the Gospel of John.

> Ye have not chosen me, but I have chosen you, and ordained you, that ye should go and bring forth fruit, and that your fruit should remain: that whatsoever ye shall ask of the Father in my name, he may give it you. (John 15:16)

The phrase, "I have chosen you," primarily speaks to us of the language of adoption. In the adoption process, the adoptee does not do the choosing. The act of choosing belongs solely to the adopter. The individual chosen by the adopter receives full rights to the adopter's name and inheritance. Also notice that believers are chosen to bear fruit that will remain. Through believers' fruit-bearing, the Father's name and values are continuously perpetuated in the earth.

The whole process of Christian adoption moves one away from bondage to sin and fear toward experiencing freedom as a child in the Kingdom of God. Fear, a by-product of sin, comes to weaken faith and keep believers from being fruitful. However, the Apostle John lets us know that the God-kind of love, which believers received at new birth, has the ability to keep us from operating in fear.

> There is no fear in love [dread does not exist], but full-grown (complete, perfect) love turns fear out of doors and expels every trace of terror! For fear brings with it the thought of punishment, and [so] he who is afraid has not reached the full maturity of love [is not yet grown into love's complete perfection]. (1 John 4:18 Amplified Bible)

Now, notice that this passage says we can grow into love's complete perfection. Once again, it is through the ministry of the Holy Spirit that we are trained and equipped to experience and grow in the God-kind of love. In sonship, the Spirit of Adoption is in the recreated spirit of every believer in order to bring each into a glorious position of intimacy and freedom. Let's look at the Apostle Paul's advice to the Galatians.

> But the fruit of the [Holy] Spirit [the work which His presence within accomplishes] is love, joy (gladness), peace, patience (an even temper, forbearance), kindness, goodness (benevolence), faithfulness, gentleness (meekness, humility), self-control (self-restraint, continence). Against such things there is no law [that can bring a charge]. (Galatians 5:22-23 Amplified Bible)

Paul declares that the evidence of the Holy Spirit working in the lives of believers is the production of holy character known as the fruit of the Spirit. As believers yield to the work of the Holy Spirit, they will produce fruit that will remain and have the ability to reflect the character of God in the earth realm. Once again, believers must yield to the wisdom of the Spirit in order for fruit production to take place in the life. In John chapter fifteen, Jesus explained to the disciples the open communication we are to experience as God's chosen ones.

> Henceforth I call you not servants; for the servant knoweth not what his lord doeth: but I have called you friends; for all things that I have heard of my Father I have made known unto you. (John 15:15)

Our relationship to Christ is on a friend to friend level of fellowship. Christ will share with us information about the Kingdom of God so that we are not ignorant of spiritual matters. Whatever Jesus hears the Father say, He has promised to share those things with His friends. Jesus explained the why of the name change: "the servant knoweth not what his lord doeth..." Masters do not share intimate details of household affairs with slaves. Only friends share details about the household's affairs and their sharing is on an open level of communication.

The God-kind of love in action is the visible language of adoption. An excellent book to read about the God-kind of love is *The New Kind of Love* by E. W. Kenyon. In this book, Kenyon gives insight into the kind of love believers are to experience as a result of being in union with Christ. Kenyon explains that God never intended for man to operate in a servile spirit; that is, to operate from a sense of inferiority and bondage. The love God has placed in believers "takes away from us the sense of inferiority and gives us the sense of our oneness with Christ."[6] "One cannot have a servile spirit and enjoy the reality of sonship."[7] "We are masters, we are conquerors, we are overcomers because we are one with Him. We have His ability, His wisdom, His strength, His love. Spiritually, we are free men. We abide in God and God abides in us."[8] All that man lost because of the fall in the Garden of Eden, Christ has restored in His union with believers; thus, believers are no longer slaves to sin but masters over it. Believers are to see themselves as dead to sin and alive unto Christ (Romans 6:11). In our union with Christ Jesus, the God-kind of love we experience trains us to speak a new language—the language befitting children of God.

In addition to this new level of open communication, we are to experience family life. Jesus did not leave us as orphans: "comfortless, desolate, bereaved, forlorn, helpless" in this world. (John14:18 paraphrased from Amplified Bible) In the new position of sons of God, we are a part of God's family. For a moment, let us consider the contrast between sonship and being an orphan. An orphan does not have a legal Father or a legal family structure. In sonship, believers are legally a part of a powerful family that is ruled by an omnipotent loving Father. Believers belong to the Kingdom of God—the domain where God is King—and have been given the power and authority to perpetuate the family's values and the family's name, Jesus, in the earth. Since the crucifixion and resurrection, everything that we do is through the power of the name of Jesus.

Why can believers speak the language of adoption? Believers can speak the language of adoption (sonship) because the enmity between God and mankind was put away

---

[6]   The New Kind of Love, p. 30
[7]   Ibid.
[8]   Ibid.

by the cross of Jesus—God is not angry with mankind. God is not angry, nor is He sitting and waiting on opportunities to explode in wrath toward believers. Through faith in Jesus' redemptive work, believers have access into the presence of a loving Father and can boldly go into His presence to obtain the help needed to operate in the dominion mandate. Every believer can enter into an intimate level of open communication with God the Father and call Him "Abba."

For many decades, the Body of Christ has reflected a faulty form of worshipping God which produced a false image of God's character. Our worship of God has reflected Him as capricious, wrathful, judgmental, and a spectator. It is because of these faulty images of God that some unbelievers have no desire to know the God of Christianity. As believers express worship toward God at this new level of intimate open communication, the true image of the Father and the Kingdom of God blankets the atmosphere and touches the hearts of others. It is this intimate level of open communication that stirs a desire in the hearts of others to become a part of the Kingdom of God.

## CHAPTER NINE

# THE BLESSINGS OF SONSHIP, PART ONE

I n the position of sons of God, there are manifold blessings which believers experience: restoration to relationship and fellowship, a new nature, a new name, a family, and an inheritance. Because the Word of God has a great deal to say about each of these blessings, I have spread the information over two chapters. Since God predestinated sonship as the legal position through which the manifold blessings of the Kingdom flow into the lives of believers, principles from previous chapters are reiterated and additional comments added to magnify the beauty and effectiveness of sonship. Now, let us take a look at each of *the blessings of sonship.*

## Restoration to Relationship and Fellowship

In sonship, believers receive restoration to relationship and fellowship with God whereby they are able to approach God, experience His love, and openly communicate with Him. From the creation story, we understand that our first parents (Adam and Eve) were created to fellowship with God at an intimate level of open communication. Adam and Eve had the capacity and ability to walk (conduct life) in the spiritual realm as well as the earthly realm. Our first parents were a portable worship center in the earth: the portal through which God's abilities were released in the earth realm. When they sinned in the Garden of Eden, the portal needful to align the earth's activities with that in heaven was closed. Instead of creation experiencing heavenly blessings, the curse prevailed in the earth. Disobedience had left Adam and Eve naked: stripped of both authority and the very nature through which God's authority flowed. Peace with God was destroyed and the joy of fellowship with God lost, leaving Adam and Eve afraid of the very God they had come to know intimately as Creator and Father.

In order for humankind to experience intimate fellowship with God again, the partition of enmity and fear had to be removed. The redemptive work of Christ Jesus removed the partition of enmity between God and fallen mankind, and restored the right to relationship and fellowship with God. Consequently, those expressing faith in Christ's redemptive work enter into restored relationship and fellowship with God. Let's take a look at a passage from the book of Ephesians:

> But God—so rich is He in His mercy! Because of and in order to satisfy the great and wonderful and intense love with which He loved us, even when we were dead (slain) by [our own] shortcomings and trespasses, He made us alive together in fellowship and in union with Christ; [He gave us the very life of Christ Himself, the same new life with which He quickened Him, for] it is by grace (His favor and mercy which you did not deserve) that you are saved (delivered from judgment and made partakers of Christ's salvation. And He raised us up together with Him and made us sit down

together [giving us joint seating with Him] in the heavenly sphere [by virtue of our being] in Christ Jesus (the Messiah, the Anointed One). (Ephesians 2:4-6 Amplified Bible)

Fallen mankind did not initiate the pursuit of fellowship with God because fear contaminated the desire to approach God in confidence. With fear influencing the heart, the only thing mankind expected to receive from God was punishment. Let us revisit the Garden of Eden for a moment.

And they heard the sound of the Lord God walking in the garden in the cool of the day, and Adam and his wife hid themselves from the presence of the Lord God among the trees of the garden. But the Lord God called to Adam and said to him. Where are you? He said, I heard the sound of You [walking] in the garden, and I was afraid because I was naked: and I hid myself. (Genesis 3:8-10 Amplified Bible)

Disobedience opened the door for fear to change the image of God in the heart. Nevertheless, God, in order to satisfy His intense love for mankind, pursued and initiated fellowship with a fearful, hiding mankind. Although Adam violated his commitment of obedience, God chose not to violate His commitment to Adam, but pursued the restoration of humankind to Himself by the voluntary sacrifice of His Son, Jesus Christ. It was indeed because *"God so loved the world"* that He gave Jesus Christ as the ransom payment for our sins. A loving Father wanted mankind back into family status; therefore, He provided a way. It is through faith in Christ's redemptive work that fallen mankind enters into a restored relationship with God whereby one becomes a child of God.

Adoption into the family of God means that believers are sons of God and have no reason to fear fellowship with Father God. In fact, believers may confidently approach God the Father, address Him in not only the more formal manner as Father, but also as "*Abba*" or Daddy! The Apostle Paul states that believers have been given the Spirit of adoption to help them cry to Father God, "*Abba,* Father!"

> For ye have not received the spirit of bondage again to fear; but ye have received the Spirit of adoption, whereby we cry, Abba, Father. (Romans 8:15)

If the Body of Christ had been abandoned or left alone in the earth, there might have been a cause to operate in the spirit of fear. However, God the Holy Spirit is here with us and dwelling inside us, therefore, believers always have the help they need in every situation. The presence of the Holy Spirit is a wonderful blessing of sonship. It is because of the presence of the Holy Spirit that believers can reject operating in the spirit of fear. As sons of God, believers have a legal right to operate in God-consciousness. Alva J. McClain states that, "On the judicial side, God adopted us as a son with every legal right as a son. He actually gave to us His own Spirit, so that we are in His family by nature, and we are so conscious of this that we call Him Father."[9]

Stay alert, and watch for signs of the old previous moral condition of slave and orphan mentality trying to invade the soul. They are a hindrance to operating in the blessings of sonship. Jesus did not leave us in slavery to sin that we should fearfully shrink from the presence of God. He set us free from bondage to sin by His own blood that we might draw nigh

---

[9]    Romans: The Gospel of God's Grace, p. 167

unto God. Faith in His redemptive work made us children of God and removes the stigma of being an orphan. Our freedom from orphan mentality is evident in the name we are trained to call Father God, that is, *Abba Father*. Therefore, stand firm in sonship rights and do not become ensnared with a yoke of bondage to fear or orphan mentality.

From the cultural backdrop of Paul's writings, we understand that slaves were not allowed to say *Abba* to a master, and orphans don't have a father. Believers who allow slave mentality or orphan mentality a place in the heart will find it very difficult, if not impossible, to refer to God the Father as *"Abba"* or Daddy. Nevertheless, they do have a legal blood bought right to address God the Father as "*Abba*, Father" and communicate with Him on an intimate open level of communication.

God's original blueprint for mankind commissioned those created in His image to exercise dominion in the earth realm and release the sound of heaven in the earth. Adam had the ability and authority to establish God's domain in the earth, thus, assuring that the activities on earth aligned with God's will. This truth gives credence to the first petition in the Lord's Prayer, "thy kingdom come on earth as it is in heaven," (Matthew 6:10). This petition in the Lord's Prayer implies that the will of God is for the heavenly realm and the earthly realm to come in alignment with one another—the latter with the former. Sonship made it possible for mankind to regain entrance into the legal position of exercising dominion in the earth and aligning the earth's activities with the heavenly realm once again.

Unfortunately, for many in the Body of Christ, sin consciousness blocks the door to experiencing the new position of adoption called *sonship*. Too many believers never allow their hearts to ascend from slave mentality into the height of being a son of God. This was the elder brother's problem in the story of the prodigal son (Luke 15:25-32). The elder brother viewed his relationship and fellowship with his father through the eyes of being a slave at the mercy of a master one had to work to please. He did not view his position in life from the standpoint of sonship. The elder brother could have experienced the blessings of sonship whenever he desired because he was his father's son. Slave mentality does not lend the heart to engage in intimate fellowship with the Father. Slave mentality does not have eyes to see God as a loving father with a heart's desire to bless His children. Adoption has liberated believers from slavery and placed them in the care of a loving Father at sonship level. Don't allow slave mentality to block this truth from your heart.

Once again, let us take a look at John 15:15, as Jesus teaches about the position of open communication to be experienced by believers:

> Henceforth I call you not servants; for the servant knoweth not what his lord doeth: but I have called you friends; for all things that I have heard of my Father I have made known unto you. (John 15:15)

The disciples understood Jesus to mean that they had free access to open communication with Him—an access that cannot be experienced at slave level. Jesus was elevating the disciples' image of their position in the Kingdom of God. The image we have of ourselves sets the boundary for the scope of authority we will release in the earth realm. Thus, it is vitally important that we see ourselves the same way God sees us.

As sons of God, believers can experience an open level of communicating with God on a daily basis. In this open level of communication, the mysteries (another name for reserved revelations) of the Kingdom are not kept hidden from believers. Jesus says to believers, "all things that I have heard of my Father I have made known unto you." We are not God's enemies, slaves, the ungodly, or strangers to the covenant, but children in the household of faith; thus, knowledge of how the Kingdom of God operates is available for our understanding. We are not to entertain ignorance of the applications of Kingdom principles, the will of God, or what is expected of us as His children. It has been given unto us, the children of God, to know the mysteries of the Kingdom of God.

> And as soon as He was alone, those who were around Him, with the Twelve [apostles], began to ask Him about the parables. And He said to them, To you has been entrusted the mystery of the kingdom of God [that is, the secret counsels of God which are hidden from the ungodly]; but for those outside [of our circle] everything becomes a parable. (Mark 4:10-11 Amplified Bible)

To the heart of those operating in sonship, there is nothing mysterious about the ways of God. Those operating in sonship understand that the Father's will is revealed in the face of Christ.

> For God Who said, Let light shine out of darkness, has shone in our hearts so as [to beam forth] the Light for the illumination of the knowledge of the majesty and glory of God [as it is manifest in the Person and is revealed] in the face of Jesus Christ (the Messiah). (Second Corinthians 4:6 Amplified Bible).

The phrase, *the face of Christ*, speaks of a position of open communication where nothing is hidden or mysterious. To be quite frank, the only true position of communication for the child of God is *face to face* with Jesus—the one who calls us "friends." Always remember that our God appointed fellowship with Jesus is not shallow. The Father wants us to know who we are and what we are expected to do as sons of God. Once again, John 15:15 records the Lord's promise of open communication with the children of God in the statement, "... for all things that I have heard of my Father I have made known unto you."

A wonderful method of experiencing intimate fellowship is to enter daily into this open level of communication with the Lord so that He may impart the Father's desires into the heart. One of the aspects of the ministry of the Holy Spirit is to take the sons of God into intimate open communication with the Lord. However, it is the responsibility of the sons of God to cooperate with the Holy Spirit as He leads.

As we engage in fellowship with the Lord, we must take note that ministering in the Father's house as *sons of God* carries more weight than ministering as a *servant*—even as a faithful servant. The author of the book of Hebrews expounds on the contrast between being a servant in the Kingdom verses being a son.

> And Moses verily was faithful in all his house, as a servant, for a testimony of those things which were to be spoken after; but Christ as a son over his own house; whose house are we, if we hold fast the confidence and the rejoicing of the hope firm unto the end. (Hebrews 3:5-6)

Let's review the contrast: Christ (the Son) was greater than Moses (the servant) because Christ as the Son is the Builder of God's house whereas Moses only performed duties in the house.

Prior to understanding this passage in Hebrews, I often pondered why the reality of God as Father seemed to evade the grasp of some believers, causing them to continuously operate in a warped image of God whereby they viewed Him as some type of angry tyrant they had to work hard to please. Through the lens of this passage, I have come to the realization that there are some in the Body of Christ who never move beyond the mentality of rendering *"service"* in the Lord's House as a means of earning God's love. They faithfully serve, but they do not grow in the intimate knowing of God or His ways. These believers are stuck in the mental rut of serving God in order to earn His love and the benefits of salvation. They operate by a spirit of fear and are satisfied with ritualistic worship that lacks a personal encounter with God, while those operating in sonship are experiencing the Father's love at an intimate level of fellowship.

Can we talk for a moment? As a child of God, do not see yourself as a servant having to do work in order to earn the Father's love. Settle in your heart the eternal truth that you belong to God; you are His offspring whom He loves dearly. As children of the Kingdom of God, we respect God the Father's authority in our lives and honor His parental right to guide us according to His divine purpose for our lives. These things we do because of our love for Him as *Abba,* Father. We never have to do them in order to earn His love. Abba Father is not an angry tyrant, but a good Father Who freely loves us with an everlasting love and wants nothing but the best for our lives. In addition, our serving one another and others is always from the position of redeeming love: we love because He first loved us. Our motives for serving in the Kingdom should never be to earn love. Serving in order to earn love is an aspect of works righteousness and a bondage we are not to allow in our lives. What is works righteousness? Works righteousness is the belief that one is justified before God and gains favor with God by doing good works. In order for the children of God to experience the blessings of sonship and reflect the true image of God in the earth realm, we will have to stay away from operating in works righteousness.

Just as some in the household of faith are ensnared by works righteousness, others are trapped in webs of guilt and condemnation. Guilt and condemnation are by-products of disobedience, and they are very hard task masters. Guilt and condemnation set the affections of the heart toward punishment as they devalue one's identity as a child of God. Looking once again at the parable of the prodigal son, being a hired servant in his father's house was the youngest son's solution to his own disobedience—it was all he felt he was worth.

> When he finally came to his senses, he said to himself, At home even the hired men have food enough to spare, and here I am, dying of hunger! I will go home to my father and say, "Father, I have sinned against both heaven and you, and I am no longer worthy of being called your son. Please take me on as a hired man." (Luke 15:17-19 NLT)

What was the father's reaction to his son's proposition? He forgave his son and took him back into fellowship position, not as a hired servant, but as a son—a living offspring with full sonship rights.

> But his father said to the servants, Quick! Bring the finest robe in the house and put it on him. Get a ring for his finger, and sandals for his feet. And kill the calf we have been fattening in the pen. We must celebrate with a feast, for this son of mine was dead and has now returned

to life. He was lost, but now he is found. So the
party began. (Luke 15:23-24 NLT)

As sons of God, *once lost but now found*, we will need to
stand firm in the liberty that comes with our sonship position
and not allow ourselves to gravitate back to the spiritual
bondage of religious servitude which flows from faulty images
and concepts. To rid the heart of condemnation and guilt
feelings one need only to repent of acts of disobedience and
receive God's forgiveness. I emphasize the word *only* because
there are no outward works one can do to earn forgiveness;
we must repent of sin, not try to earn our way out of it. We
are called to show forth "fruits of repentance," that is, our
lifestyle is to demonstrate that we believe God has forgiven
us and we have received His forgiveness. Our next action is
to stand in the reality of that forgiveness. In the words of the
Apostle Paul,

Stand fast therefore in the liberty wherewith
Christ hath made us free, and be not entangled
again with the yoke of bondage. (Galatians 5:1)

The forgiven *"stand fast"* in the liberty that comes with
being forgiven and they do not allow themselves to become
entangled again with the yoke of deception sin brings.
Those who stand fast in liberty experience the blessing of
relationship and fellowship with God and are able to reflect
the image of a loving forgiving God in the earth realm—an
image many need to see and embrace.

### A New Nature

Another blessing of sonship is the eternal truth that all
the children receive a new nature. The Bible teaches that all

who are in Christ Jesus possess a new nature. The sons of God have been set apart, consecrated, and possess the very nature of God in Christ Jesus.

> Therefore if any person is [ingrafted] in Christ (the Messiah) he is a new creation (a new creature altogether); the old [previous moral and spiritual condition] has passed away. Behold, the fresh and new has come! (2 Corinthians 5:17 Amplified Bible)

Prior to faith in the redemptive work of Jesus Christ, our moral and spiritual condition was *"as filthy rags,"* for all had sinned and come short of the glory God had originally created in mankind (Romans 3:10-16). Nevertheless, once an individual accepts Jesus as Lord and Savior, that previous moral and spiritual *"filthy rag"* condition is discarded and that individual's nature is made fresh and new. Our God is the God of a fresh new start!

In this fresh new start, the individual has been given the righteous nature of God in Christ Jesus. It is because of this miraculous work of the Father that we have been placed in sonship position and are now called the sons of God. The Apostle Paul stated, "For our sake He made Christ [virtually] to be sin Who knew no sin, so that in and through Him we might become [endued with, viewed as being in, and examples of] the righteousness of God [what we ought to be, approved and acceptable and in right relationship with Him by His goodness]." (2 Corinthians 5:21 Amplified Bible) The new nature of the recreated spirit equips every believer with the capacity to reflect the image (nature) of God in the earth realm.

## CHAPTER TEN

# THE BLESSINGS OF SONSHIP, PART TWO

## A New Name

In sonship, there is the blessing of bearing the family's name and having the right to dispense the authority of that name in the earth. These two blessings show the two-fold goal of adoption which is: (1) to assure that there will be an heir to perpetuate the family's name and (2) continue the distribution of the family's values in the earth.

In chapter six, I discussed the two predominant names that belong to believers through adoption: *children of God* and *sons of God*. In addition to these two names, believers are called by several other biblical names which speak to us of the effects of the new nature indwelling the recreated spirit. Let us take a look at a few of these names:

- **Believers are called God's beloved ones and saints:** "To [you then] all God's beloved ones in Rome, called to be saints and designated for a consecrated life: Grace and spiritual blessing and peace be yours from God our Father and from the Lord Jesus Christ." (Romans 1:7 Amplified Bible) The new birth experience translated believers from the kingdom of darkness into the Kingdom of Light (Colossians 1:12-14). In the kingdom of darkness, every individual is a sinner by nature. However, because of the holy nature within the believer's recreated spirit, all are called saints in the Kingdom of Light. This name is ascribed to every believer because of the holy nature in the recreated spirit and is not based upon good works or deeds accomplished. For some believers, sin consciousness blocks the understanding of this name change. Nevertheless, the Scripture testify that believers are *blameless, consecrated,* and *holy* by virtue of the new nature within the recreated spirit. God chose us because He loved us and wanted us to experience His love (Colossians 3:12). In order for us to have the freedom to experience His love, our nature had to be changed. A change in nature constitutes a change in name. Through faith in the redemptive work of Christ, our nature and name have changed. It is in the beloved Son, Jesus Christ, that we now live, move, and have our being as *saints* in the Kingdom of God (Acts 17:28).

- **Believers are called the church (assembly) of God and people of God:** "To the church (assembly) of God which is in Corinth, to those consecrated and purified and made holy in Christ Jesus, [who are] selected and called to be saints (God's people), together with all those who in any place call upon and give honor to the name of our Lord Jesus Christ, both their Lord and ours." (1 Corinthians 1:2 Amplified Bible) Believers were purchased, redeemed with the blood of Jesus. Through faith in this purchase, we have been made God's people—believers belong to God as His very own people (1 Corinthians 6:20).

- **Believers are called citizens of the Kingdom of God:** "Therefore you are no longer outsiders (exiles, migrants, and aliens, excluded from the rights of citizens), but you now share citizenship with the saints (God's own people, consecrated and set apart for Himself); and you belong to God's [own] household," (Ephesians 2:19 Amplified Bible). The Kingdom of God has a governmental structure with laws which regulate the privileges its citizens are expected to obey and enjoy. As citizens of the Kingdom of God, we live by the law of love as we walk by the principles of faith (Ephesians 5:1-2).

- **Believers are called children of the Light:** "For once you were darkness, but now you are light in the Lord; walk as children of Light [lead the lives of those native-born to the Light]." (Ephesians 5:8 Amplified Bible) The phrase, *"Walk as children of the Light,"* means to reject the evil way and live a righteous holy lifestyle. This change in the believer's attitude toward evil takes place by daily yielding to the ministry of the Holy Spirit. The Holy Spirit trains believers to move from evil practices and replace them with responding to everyday life's situations as Christ would respond to them.

- **Believers are called God's chosen ones, God's picked representatives:** "Clothe yourselves therefore, as God's own chosen ones (His own picked representatives), [who are] purified and holy and well-beloved [by God Himself, by putting on behavior marked by] tenderhearted pity and mercy, kind feeling, a lowly opinion of yourselves, gentle ways, [and] patience [which is tireless and long-suffering, and has the power to endure whatever comes, with good temper." (Colossians 3:12 Amplified Bible) The phrase *"clothe yourselves"* speaks to us of aligning our attitudes with the new nature of the recreated spirit. Living by the nature of the recreated spirit is new terrain for believers; therefore, Jesus sent the Holy Spirit to help with that task. The Holy Spirit prompts and guides believers into the right application of the written Word of God. The evidence that the believer is yielding to the guidance of the Holy Spirit will be the new behavior patterns mentioned in this passage (tenderhearted pity and mercy, kind feeling, etc.).

The point we are making is that biblical names help us locate our identity and purpose in life. Knowing one's spiritual identity and purpose gives a sense of direction for one's life. Throughout the New Testament, believers are identified as having the righteous, holy nature of God. The possession of this new nature equips the sons of God with the ability to reflect the image of God in the earth realm. Just like the moon reflects the light which comes from the sun, believers, through their union with Christ Jesus, are to be a reflection of God's holy nature while they live in the earth realm.

Before we leave this section, let's take a look at one more name which identifies who we are as sons of God. Second Corinthians 5:20 states, "So we are Christ's ambassadors, God making His appeal as it were through us. We [as Christ's personal representatives] beg you for His sake to lay hold of the divine favor [now offered you] and be reconciled to God." (Amplified Bible) Ambassadors are authorized representatives of the government that sent them, therefore, do not represent self. Likewise it is with the believer. As sons of God, we do not express our own opinions for we are ambassadors of the Kingdom of God. In our face to face communication with the Lord, whatever message we hear from Him is the message we give to the people. In that manner, believers will always be equipped to reflect the true image of God in the earth realm.

There is more depth to sonship than getting one's name in the Lamb's Book of Life and, as some believe, waiting to go to heaven to get away from the adversities the devil brings. Through sonship, believers are given the right to exercise power and authority over all the ill will of the devil. Looking back at Genesis, we understand that Adam was God's ambassador in the earth realm. Adam was given a dominion mandate to subdue and exercise authority in the earth for the good of mankind and for God's purposes.

> And God blessed them and said to them, Be fruitful, multiply, and fill the earth, and subdue it [using all its vast resources in the service of God and man]; and have dominion over the fish of the sea, the birds of the air, and over every living creature that moves upon the earth. (Genesis 1:28 Amplified Bible)

In mankind's fallen state, man's abuse of the dominion mandate reached levels of depravity that took mankind farther and farther away from God's original plan. However, the story does not end there! Faith in the redemptive work of Christ Jesus restores the legal right to once again exercise dominion in the earth realm in accordance with God's original plan. With this restored right comes the command to be empowered for service as an ambassador of Christ.

Now, keep in mind that the goal of the original mandate was to give mankind the legal right to exercise authority in the earth for the good of mankind and the purposes of God. With this backdrop in mind, hear the sound of the lost crying out for help and understand that only eternal life has the solution to their cries. In view of the condition of the lost, believers were commanded to be empowered with the ability needful to set at liberty those in bondage to the deceptions of sin and the devil. Once again, it is the cry of the lost that prompted Paul to write, "So we are Christ's ambassadors, God making His appeal as it were through us. We [as Christ's personal representatives] beg you for His sake to lay hold of the divine favor [now offered you] and be reconciled to God."

The summons to become empowered for service in the Kingdom of God, and operate in the earth with power and authority, comes from the Lord Jesus Christ Himself. Jesus declared that if anyone is thirsty, they need to come to Him and drink. He promised that whoever drinks the water He has to give will become a dispenser of that same water. Those who drink of the water Jesus gives become empowered for service as ambassadors in the Kingdom of God.

> Now on the final and most important day of the Feast, Jesus stood, and He cried in a loud voice, If any man is thirsty, let him come to Me and drink! He who believes in Me [who cleaves to and trusts in and relies on Me] as the Scripture has said, From his innermost being shall flow [continuously] springs and rivers of living water. But He was speaking here of the Spirit, Whom those who believed (trusted, had faith) in Him were afterward to receive, For the [Holy] Spirit had not yet been given, because Jesus was not yet glorified (raised to honor). (John 7:37-39 Amplified Bible)

The prerequisite for receiving this supply of living water from Jesus is one must be thirsty for truth—for God's reality. Jesus declared that those who are thirsty for truth need not go to any other source for satisfaction. Those desiring truth need to *come to Him* and *believe in Him*. The miraculous will happen to all who are thirsty and come to Jesus for satisfaction: a continuous stream of living water will flow from all who seek satisfaction from the Lord Jesus Christ. This passage is a direct reference to the ministry of the Holy Spirit empowering the sons of God with dynamic power and might. Jesus spoke of this aspect of the Holy Spirit's ministry before ascending to the right hand of the Father:

> Do not leave Jerusalem until the Father sends you what he promised. Remember, I have told you about this before. John baptized with water, but in just a few days you will be baptized with the Holy Spirit. (Acts 1:4-5 NLT)

The disciples were given the charge to preach the Kingdom to the utter ends of the earth, but were told not to go on the assignment until they were endued with power. Likewise, the household of faith (the Church) operates in that same charge. A way to operate in the dominion mandate has been restored and the sons of God have been given the capacity to fulfill it. In our implementation of the dominion mandate, let us move forward and couple the restored capacity of the recreated spirit with the empowerment of the Holy Spirit, just as the first disciples were instructed to do by the Lord.

The instructions given to the disciples were very explicit and hold true for us today. Every believer is to be empowered by the Holy Spirit with the power and might needful to proclaim the Kingdom of God and destroy the works of the devil. Believers are to move from salvation at the foot of the Cross to the "upper room" empowerment of Pentecost.

Throughout the Book of Acts, there is biblical evidence that the Pentecostal empowerment made a difference in the discharge of Christian service. For example, the empowerment of Pentecost changed a cowardly Peter into a bold orator who proclaimed Christ and 3,000 souls were ushered into the

Kingdom of God. The empowerment of the Spirit changed Saul of Tarsus into the Apostle Paul, who operated in unusual signs and wonders during his ministry. We all are thankful for the revelations that were imparted to Paul in the writing of the epistles.

The New Testament dominion mandate (which basically gives instructions on how to fulfill the original mandate) is located in the Gospels of Matthew and Mark. Let us take a look at these instructions. From the Gospel of Matthew, we find what is referred to as the Great Commission of the Church (our family):

> Jesus came and told his disciples, "I have been given complete authority in heaven and on earth. Therefore, go and make disciples of all the nations, baptizing them in the name of the Father and the Son and the Holy Spirit. Teach these new disciples to obey all the commands I have given you. And be sure of this: I am with you always even to the end of the age."
> (Matthew 28:18-20 NLT)

This passage clearly identifies Jesus' delegation of authority to the family to continue His earthly ministry of making disciples of all nations. However, there are a few more specifics recorded in the Gospel of Mark:

> Go into all the world and preach the Good News to everyone, everywhere. Anyone who believes and is baptized will be saved. But anyone who refuses to believe will be condemned. These signs will accompany those who believe. They will cast out demons in my name; and they will speak new languages. They will be able

to handle snakes with safety, and if they drink anything poisonous, it won't hurt them. They will be able to place their hands on the sick and heal them. (Mark 16:15-18 NLT)

As ambassadors of the household of faith, believers have been given the authority to preach the *"Good News to everyone, everywhere"* and to destroy the works of the devil through the power of signs and wonders.

The authority and power Adam lost through disobedience, Jesus regained by His obedience to the Father's will. The statement, *"I have been given complete authority in Heaven and on the earth,"* speaks volumes about the fullness of all believers' sonship rights. Let's take a look at a prayer the Apostle Paul prayed over the believers:

> I pray that you will begin to understand the incredible greatness of his power for us who believe him. This is the same mighty power that raised Christ from the dead and seated him in the place of honor at God's right hand in the heavenly realms. Now he is far above any ruler or authority or power or leader or anything else in this world or in the world to come. And God has put all things under the authority of Christ, and he gave him this authority for the benefit of the church. And the church is his body, it is filled by Christ, who fills everything everywhere with his presence. (Ephesians 1:19-23 NLT)

The authority Christ has is for the *"benefit of the church,"* and fills believers with His very presence. This flow of authority gives credence to the statement, *"I am with you always even to the end of the age,"* because His power and presence go hand in hand. The fullness of sonship rights is experienced when one becomes a dispenser of the authority that is invested in the obedient Son, Christ Jesus—not when we get to heaven, but while we are here on the earth.

As sons of God fulfilling our ambassadorship, waiting on instructions from the Lord and listening to obey His voice are essential to operating in His power and authority in the earth realm. Isaiah expounds on the significance of the two actions in relations to being thirsty for the things of God:

> WAIT and listen, everyone who is thirsty! Come to the waters; and he who has no money, come, buy and eat! Yes, come, buy [priceless, spiritual] wine and milk without money and without price [simply for the self-surrender that accepts the blessing]. Why do you spend your money for that which is not bread, and your earnings for what does not satisfy? Hearken diligently to Me, and eat what is good, and let your soul delight itself in fatness [the profuseness of spiritual joy] Incline your ear [submit and consent to the divine will] and come to Me; hear, and your soul will revive; and I will make an everlasting covenant. (Isaiah 55:1-3 Amplified Bible)

The condition of thirst is like the indicator light on the dashboard of a car: it is a warning that something is out of order and in need of maintenance. Spiritual thirst implies that the heart is longing for answers to satisfy its deep innermost cravings. The word, *listen,* means to position one's heart with a desire to hear what God has to say. This word implies that there is a *"want to"* and a *"willingness"* motivating the heart to hear and understand what is being said. Where there is no willingness in the heart to hear and understand, the spiritual ears close down and the door to the heart is shut. Several times in the Book of Revelation, the Church is instructed to hear and understand: "Anyone who is willing to hear should listen to the Spirit and understand what the Spirit is saying to the churches." (2:7, 11, 17, 29; 3:6, 13, 22)[10] Although these instructions were written to specific churches, the message stands true for the Church today. If the sons of God are to reflect the true image of God in the earth realm, it is imperative that we *"listen to the Spirit and understand what the Spirit is saying to the churches."*

There are so many voices in the world offering a horrific amount of *dead stuff* for answers. The passage in Isaiah asks, "Why waste time and effort seeking after things that will not satisfy the spiritual yearning of your soul?" In short, one needs to stop, think, and count the cost! What did it really cost you not to wait and listen to what Jesus was saying to you personally? For too many people, it cost far too much, especially when what was purchased only devoured their lives. Praise God, Jesus gives freely to those who are thirsty. Jesus gives *"water"* that will revive the soul and lead one to an eternal relationship with Him. Jesus, as the Living Truth, has the eternal supply of water (truth about the Father) that is needful to satisfy the soul.

There is always a blessing flowing from waiting and listening to obey the Lord. The amazing aspect about this passage in Isaiah is that you don't have to be rich or famous in order to partake of the blessing offered. The blessing that will quench mankind's thirst and satisfy the soul can be obtained by the simple act of self-surrender to the voice of the Lord.

---

[10] New Living Translation, p. 1127-1129

## A Family

In sonship, there is the blessing of being a member of a very large family which operates in power and authority in the earth. According to Ephesians 2:19, believers are *"fellow citizens with the saints, and of the household of God."* In most countries, especially those with governmental structures which inspire freedom, citizens have rights and privileges. As a citizen of the household of God, believers have been accepted into full family rights and privileges. These rights and privileges are superior to and take precedence over all others in the earth realm.

Family was God's unique idea. The archives of Biblical history testify that there is no better group of people to effect positive change in this world than the family. In addition, hindsight has taught us that to destroy the family structure of a culture is to set in motion a course which leads to the decay of moral values and ultimately chaos. For this cause, there are spiritual rules and principles governing our family relationship and unity in fellowship which must be guarded and obeyed:

1. Ephesians 3:17-19 states, "That Christ may dwell in your hearts by faith; that ye, being rooted and grounded in love, may be able to comprehend with all saints what is the breadth, and length, and depth, and height; and to know the love of Christ, which passeth knowledge, that ye might be filled with all the fulness of God." As a member of the family of God, faith, love, and fellowship are principles that set the boundaries of our interaction with each other and the Lord. Purpose in your heart to respect these principles and tenderheartedly handle them with high esteem. Stay away from strife, arrogance, and lust because these three vices open the door for other evil practices to

enter and destroy the unity of the family. They are thieves who come to steal, kill, and destroy the family of God.

2. James 1:18-19 states, "Of his own will begat he us with the word of truth, that we should be a kind of firstfruits of his creatures. Wherefore, my beloved brethren, let every man be swift to hear, slow to speak, slow to wrath..." As sons of God, we are God's increase from the Seed, Christ Jesus, Who was planted according to God's determined plan. According to the law of sowing and reaping recorded in Genesis chapter one, every seed produces after His own kind. Therefore, our manner of conversation and behavior should look like the character of the Seed that was planted—Christ Jesus. As we yield our hearts to obey the prompting of the Holy Spirit, and let the Word of God dwell in us richly, our character will become nothing less than the full character found in Christ Jesus. As our souls possess more of His character, we will become vessels that are *"swift to hear, slow to speak, and slow to wrath."*

3. First Corinthians 12:12 and 20-23 states, "For as the body is one, and hath many members, and all the members of that one body, so also is Christ...But now are they many members, yet but one body. And the eye cannot say unto the hand, I have no need of thee: nor again the head to the feet, I have no need of you. Nay, much more those members of the body, which seem to be more feeble, are necessary; And those members of the body, which we think to be less honourable, upon these we bestow more abundant honour, and our uncomely parts have more abundant comeliness. For our comely parts have no need: but God hath tempered the body together, having given

more abundant honour to that part which lacked: That there should be no schism in the body; but that the members should have the same care one for another." Unlike the ungodly spirit that rested on Cain, we are our brother's keeper. We are to always keep in mind that God has arranged each believer in the Body of Christ (our family) according to His wisdom. We do well to remember that our family is a living organism with a multitude of skin colors, but only one blood flows through our spiritual veins and joins us together and that is the blood of Jesus Christ. It was through faith in His blood that each of us became a member of the family of God regardless of race or skin color. In Christ all the children stand equal before the Father because the same blood paid for their adoption into His family. Let us not make *schisms* in the Body, but tenderly care one for another.

4. First Peter 3:8-9 states, "Finally, be ye all of one mind, having compassion one of another, love as brethren, be pitiful, be courteous: Not rendering evil for evil, or railing for railing: but contrariwise blessing; knowing that ye are thereunto called, that ye should inherit a blessing." We are to be friendly and merciful in our attitude toward one another. Peradventure anyone should become angry and speak harsh words, don't retaliate or rail back, but bless with a word of encouragement and forgiveness.

## An Inheritance

In sonship, there is the blessing of receiving an inheritance. Our inheritance comes from God, and was given to us at new birth. Let's confirm this truth with the Word of God.

Furthermore, because of Christ, we have received an inheritance from God, for he chose us from the beginning, and all things happen just as he decided long ago...I pray that your hearts will be flooded with light so that you can understand the wonderful future he has promised to those he called. I want you to realize what a rich and glorious inheritance he has given to his people. (Ephesians 1:11 18 NLT)

Giving thanks unto the Father, which hath made us meet to be partakers of the inheritance of the saints in light: Who hath delivered us from the power of darkness, and hath translated us into the kingdom of his dear Son: In whom we have redemption through his blood, even the forgiveness of sins. (Colossians 1:12-14)

Every son of God is a "partaker of the inheritance of the saints in light" because of the shed blood of Jesus. Our inheritance is not something we earned or even deserved. The redemptive work of Jesus Christ, and our faith in that redeeming work, "made us fit to share the portion which is the inheritance of the saints."[11] Whatever inheritance that belongs to Christ also belongs to the believers. Christ is heir of all things (Hebrews 1:2) and through adoption, God has made believers joint heirs with Christ Jesus (Romans 8:17).

It is through our union with Christ that we are positioned in our inheritance and have been given the pledge or guarantee of the manifestation of the complete inheritance.

---

[11] Amplified Bible: Colossians 1:12

Furthermore, because of Christ, we have received an inheritance from God, for he chose us from the beginning, and all things happen just as he decided long ago. God's purpose was that we who were the first to trust in Christ should praise our glorious God. And now you also have heard the truth, the Good News that God saves you. And when you believed in Christ, he identified you as his own by giving you the Holy Spirit, whom he promised long ago. The Spirit is God's guarantee that he will give us everything he promised and that he has purchased us to be his own people. (Ephesians 1:11-14a NLT)

The Father starts all the children with the Holy Spirit as (1) the assurance or witness that each believer belongs to the Father as His purchased child and (2) the guarantee that all the promises of God are "yes" and "amen" in Christ Jesus our Lord. The Holy Spirit also prompts believers to enter into a personal parent-child relationship with the Father by training believers to refer to God as Abba, Father. As the sons of God commune with the Holy Spirit, trust and a continuous level of strong active faith is cultivated in the heart. In the same manner that Jesus turned water into wine, communion with the Holy Spirit gives Him an opportunity to transform the knowledge we gained from our study of the written Word into the reality of the Living Word, Christ Jesus, in our hearts. In other words, the Holy Spirit gives us the right interpretation and application of the written Word as He makes Christ a reality in our hearts (John 15:26; 16:13-14). Make every effort to learn about the ministry of the Holy Spirit because it is through His ministry that believers grow and are strengthened in the faith (Jude verse 20).

Eternal Life is a part of all believers' inheritance (Matthew 19:29 and Titus 3:7). The Greek words for eternal life are *aiōniŏs* (perpetual) and *zōē* (life). Eternal life, or everlasting life, is the same quality of perpetual life that is in God; thus, we refer to it as the God-kind of life. The only way for fallen mankind to experience eternal life is through the new birth experience. In the new birth experience, fallen individuals are given a new nature—one that is righteous and holy. The Apostle Paul states that "if any man be in Christ Jesus he is a new creature," (2 Corinthians 5:17). In the fallen state, sin damaged mankind's spiritual nature beyond repair; therefore, it must be discarded and replaced with the same quality of life that is found in Christ Jesus. The means of obtaining this new birth experience is through faith in the redemptive work of Jesus. Through a personal confession of faith, each believer receives a new spiritual nature and is reconciled to God. According to John 3:16, it was the love of God pursuing mankind with this great gracious gift of eternal life: "For God so loved the world that he gave his only begotten Son, that whosoever believeth on him shall not perish but have everlasting life." Whosoever confesses faith in the redemptive work of Jesus Christ has everlasting life by virtue of the new nature in the recreated spirit (Romans 10:9-10).

Eternal life is a new creature present tense reality with futuristic implications. For many decades, the Church has failed to grasp this truth and has viewed eternal life as a futuristic act of God—something believers receive when they arrive in heaven. In addition, the Church at large has not understood the scope of salvation as denoted in the Greek word *sozo* from which the English word *saved* was translated. The Greek word *sozo* means "to save i.e. deliver or protect (lit. or fig.): -heal, preserve, save (self), do well, be (make) whole."[12]

---

[12] Strong's Exhaustive Concordance, #4982

As you can see, the Greek word covers much more than the futuristic state we have restricted the English translation to mean. With these doctrinal errors at work in the Church, the biblical truths about the inheritance of believers became blurred and ineffective in the earthly life. Since this lack of clarity exists, let us plow through the Word of God and review some of the passages regarding the present and futuristic unveiling of the inheritance in order that we might clearly understand what belongs to us right now.

Deliverance belongs to us now. The Word of God says that we have been delivered from the power of darkness and translated into the Kingdom of light (Colossians 1:12-13). This is every believer's entrance into the inheritance. This initial deliverance brings with it the assurance of deliverance from all the ills of the adversary as a part of our inheritance. From the Old Testament we learn that "many are the afflictions of the righteous but the Lord delivers such a one from them all." (Psalm 34:19) From Second Timothy 4:18, we get a glimpse of the Lord's delivering and preserving power at work in the Apostle Paul's life: "[And indeed] the Lord will certainly deliver and draw me to Himself from every assault of evil, He will preserve and bring me safe unto His heavenly kingdom. To Him be the glory forever and ever. Amen (so be it)." (Amplified Bible) Peter recounts several events, from the Old Testament, of the Lord's delivering the righteous from evil and concludes this narrative with a bold assurance that the Lord will continue to do the same for the New Testament believers: "Now if [all these things are true, then be sure] the Lord knows how to rescue the godly out of temptations and trials, and how to keep the ungodly under chastisement until the day of judgment and doom," (2 Peter 2:9 Amplified Bible). As a part of the believer's inheritance, deliverance from evil in the earthly realm is a promise and is to be expected whenever any believer is confronted by evil.

The name of Jesus belongs to us now. All that Christ has inherited is represented in His name. As joint heirs with Jesus Christ, believers have access to this inheritance (Hebrews 1:4, Ephesians 2:6). There is power in the Name of Jesus and the sons of God have been commissioned to use this family name as they exercise authority in the earth realm (John 14:13-14). Peter declared that the crippled man at the Gate Beautiful was healed through the power of the Name of Jesus: "And His name, through and by faith in His name, has made this man whom you see and recognize well and strong. [Yes] the faith which is through and by Him [Jesus] has given the man this perfect soundness [of body] before all of you." (Acts 3:16 Amplified Bible) Once again, Peter speaks concerning the healed man from the Gate Beautiful and declares that "there is no other name under heaven given among men by and in which we must be saved." (Acts 4:12b Amplified Bible) As we previously discussed, the word *saved* comes from the Greek word *sozo* and means more than being born again. Peter is making a reference to the crippled man being made whole: delivered from sickness and receiving physical soundness. There is no other name by which anyone can be delivered from sickness and made completely whole. Through faith in the Name of Jesus, the realm of the miraculous is opened and the goodness of God is released in the earth.

Grace belongs to us now. As Christians remain vitally united to Christ, the power flowing from His resurrection flows to believers to assist with victorious living in the earth realm. We often refer to this power as resurrection power, yet not fully understanding or acknowledging that resurrection power is a form of grace. For decades, the Church was taught only one aspect of grace and that is unmerited favor. We thank God for the teachings on grace being God's unmerited favor, however, there is a power aspect to grace. As accurate teaching on the ministry of the Holy Spirit became available, the Church became acquainted with the other aspects of grace.

- From James 4:6, we learn that grace is God's delivering power at work: "But He gives us more and more grace (power of the Holy Spirit, to meet this evil tendency and all others fully). That is why He says, God sets Himself against the proud and haughty, but gives grace [continually] to the lowly (those who are humble enough to receive it." (Amplified Bible)
- From Ephesians 2:5, we learn that God's power (grace) is at work in our deliverance from the kingdom of darkness: "Even when we were dead (slain) by [our own] shortcomings and trespasses, He made us alive together in fellowship and in union with Christ; [He gave us the very life of Christ Himself, the same new life with which He quickened Him, for] it is by grace (His favor and mercy which you did not deserve) that you are saved (delivered from judgment and made partakers of Christ's salvation)." (Amplified Bible) Consequently, believers are expected to meet with God at the throne of grace and receive the help they need: "So let us come boldly to the throne of our gracious God. There we will receive his mercy, and we will find grace to help us when we need it." (NLT)

If the sons of God are to produce anything that is Kingdom productive, it will be accomplished by the power of God working through them and that power is grace.

Peace is our present reality—it belongs to us now. Jesus told the disciples that He was leaving them a peace which was uniquely different from what the world had to offer:

"Peace I leave with you; My [own] peace I now give and bequeath to you. Not as the world gives do I give to you. Do not let your hearts be troubled, neither let them be afraid. [Stop allowing yourselves to be agitated and disturbed; and do not permit yourselves to be fearful and intimidated and cowardly and unsettled.]" (John 14:27 Amplified Bible)

In the believer's union with Christ, when allowed, there is an assurance of the Father's love and care penetrating the heart. By definition of the Greek word used for peace, believers have been "set at one again"[13] with the Father and can "rest quietly"[14] in the assurance of His love, free from agitation or intimidation.

The presence of God belongs to us now. However, there is both a present and futuristic promise of believers personally experiencing the presence of God: in the earth realm and in the heavenly realm. Regarding the earth realm, Jesus promised that the Father would send the Holy Spirit to represent Him and remain with us forever (John 14:16, 26). From the Amplified Bible version of Hebrews 13:5, God's promise of unwavering personal help can be clearly understood: " ...for He [God] Himself has said, I will not in any way fail you nor give you up nor leave you without support. [I will] not [I will] not, [I will] not in any degree leave you helpless nor forsake nor let [you] down (relax My hold on you)! [Assuredly not!]" Regarding the heavenly realm, believers will spend eternity in God's presence (1 Thessalonians 4:17).

Answered prayer belongs to us now. God has promised to hear-to-answer every petition which aligns with His will

---

13 Strong's Exhaustive Concordance
14 Ibid.

114

with a yes and Amen (1 Peter 3:12, James 5:16). Believers need to expect God the Father to answer prayer and not be double-minded about the Father's love and concern for His children. Never approach prayer with orphan mentality— believers have a legitimate spiritual Father. For this reason, Jesus taught the disciples to pray, "Our Father, which art in heaven..." (Matthew 6:9a) In addition, as believers pray in faith, the Holy Spirit comes to help us offer prayer (Romans 8:26).

All spiritual blessings in the heavenly realm belong to the sons of God as present tense blessings. As joint heirs with Jesus Christ, believers are blessed with every spiritual blessing which is in Christ Jesus our Lord, (Ephesians 1:3, Colossians 3:24). As believers come into clearer understanding of this present tense reality, the ability to reflect the true image of God in the earth realm increases.

## CHAPTER ELEVEN

# THE LIBERTY OF SONSHIP

I n chapter nine, a few highlights about staying away from the spirit of fear were discussed. However, for this chapter, we want to delve deeper into the study of how fear hinders us from operating in our sonship rights.

Since we have been given authority to rule in the earth, we are to stay away from operating in the spirit of fear because fear hinders our ability to rule wisely. Operating in fear causes believers to look for answers in the reasoning of the mind rather than seek the wisdom of God. Fear brings torment and hopelessness and hinders the spiritual ability of believers to live by faith. For that reason, believers are to move away from listening to the voice of fear and stand firmly in faith. In the Book of Galatians, Paul wrote, "In [this] freedom Christ has made us free [and completely liberated us]; stand fast then, and do not be hampered and held ensnared and submit again to a yoke of slavery [which you have once put off]." (Galatians 5:1 Amplified Bible) Always remember that our union with Christ gives us a spirit of power, love, and a sound mind (2 Timothy 1:7).

There are two very weighty reasons why believers don't have to yield to the spirit of fear. The first reason is that the righteous nature within the recreated human spirit releases the ability to stand in the Father's presence without feeling fearful or guilty. Because of the righteous nature within our recreated spirit, we can come boldly to the throne of grace and receive whatever help we need (Hebrews 4:13). We refer to this bold ability as righteous consciousness. Sin consciousness produces feelings of fear and guilt which hinder the ability to enter into intimate fellowship with the Father and exercise authority in the earth realm. Righteous consciousness helps believers to freely enter into loving, intimate fellowship with the Father at a child-like faith level which yields a greater release of obedience to the Father's will. Righteous consciousness stimulates faith and creates a portal for the release of authority and power in the earth realm.

The second reason believers don't have to yield to the spirit of fear is because the Spirit of adoption within the recreated spirit cries from a position of intimate affectionate love, affirming that believers have been accepted into the beloved and are indeed God's very own children (Romans 8:16). This confident assurance moves believers away from feelings of receiving wrath from God to the expectation of a peaceful, trusting relationship with God. It is this confident assurance which continuously testifies that believers do not have to yield to the voice of fear. The Spirit of adoption helps believers to see God as a peaceful loving Father Who wants only good for the lives of His children. Let me pull aside and expound on this aspect of the ministry of the Holy Spirit called the Spirit of adoption.

The ministry of the Holy Spirit is vital to entering into and maintaining a faith relationship with God. Unfortunately, many believers know very little about His ministry to the Church. When we were babes in the Lord, our greatest assurance that God loved us was "the Bible tells me so." We sang, "Yes Jesus Loves Me," and hoped for things to get better in the "sweet by and by." We knew it was written in John 3:16 that God loved us and sent Jesus to die for us. Yet, our image of God's love was so marred by viewing Him as a wrathful capricious God that we derived very little benefit from our little song. In those days, very few of us knew or understood the truth recorded in Romans 8:15 and 16. Let us take a look at these verses:

> For [the Spirit which] you have now received [is] not a spirit of slavery to put you once more in bondage to fear, but you have received the Spirit of adoption [the Spirit producing sonship] in [the bliss of] which we cry Abba (Father)! Father! The Spirit Himself [thus] testifies together with our own spirit, [assuring us] that we are children of God. (Amplified Bible)

In every believer's recreated spirit there is a living testimony that they belong to God and are loved by God as His very own child. As believers engage in sweet communion with the Holy Spirit, this testimony becomes a reality in their souls and a daily truth which governs the life. It is through sweet communion with the Holy Spirit that the love of the Father begins to saturate areas in the soul and casts out phobias, agitations, intimidations, and anything else which was instigated by the spirit of fear. The God-kind of love begins to set up love stations of power and authority in the soul as it pulls down strongholds in the mind which were built by the spirit of fear.

If this is true, why are so many believers afraid of adversity and feel there is little or no hope of change when adversity comes? The answer to this question is believers must learn to be led by the Holy Spirit and not the spirit of fear: learn to walk by faith and not by sight or any thoughts which exalt themselves against the true knowledge of God. The Holy Spirit teaches believers about the Father's love and testifies with our recreated human spirit that we have been fully accepted by God as His very own beloved children. Believers need to act on the Spirit's testimony and not lean to their own understanding as to the outcome of life's challenges. The Spirit of Adoption teaches believers to never put a period where God has placed a comma.

If we walk by sight, our hearts will entertain the spirit of fear and close the door to intimate fellowship with the Father. In short, we will fellowship with the problem and not with the solution—God. As God's own beloved children, we communicate with God through the recreated human spirit by the means of faith; that is, by the leaning of the entire human personality on God in absolute trust in His counsel, power, and goodness. The walk of faith will always bring the sons of God face to face with righteous consciousness, intimate fellowship with the Father, and victorious living in the earth realm. It is through the lifestyle of faith that believers are able to stand firm in liberty and reflect the true image of God in the earth.

## CHAPTER TWELVE

# SONSHIP DUTIES

As sons of God, believers are to perpetuate the Father's name and Kingdom values in their everyday practical living. In Matthew chapter five, Jesus taught that believers are both salt and light. The believers' duties of perpetuating the Father's name and Kingdom values are contained within these teachings. Let us study these passages in order to gain insight into how to perform our sonship duties.

> You are the salt of the earth, but if salt has lost its tastes (its strength, its quality), how can its saltness be restored? It is not good for anything any longer but to be thrown out and trodden underfoot by men. (Matthew 5:13 Amplified Bible)

Jesus said that believers are salt. In the natural, salt is used to season, preserve, and heal. Likewise, believers are sent to *season* the lost with the knowledge of the Kingdom of God and the Lordship of Jesus Christ. As believers minister, the information they give should *preserve* lives and not contaminate the hearts or minds of the listeners with false teaching. For this reason, it is necessary for believers to be led by the Spirit of Truth (another name for the Holy Spirit) while proclaiming the Kingdom of God. Healing will flow to those who hear and accept the message of Truth. The Gospel of Jesus Christ is the message believers are to declare to others. Paul declares that we are not to be ashamed of this message because therein is the power of salvation to everyone who believes it with a personal conviction of its reality (Romans 1:16). As believers perform the duty of being salt, habitual sweet communion with the Holy Spirit helps to maintain strength and quality of character so that believers are never without a fresh supply of salt. Now, let us take a look at why believers are called light.

> You are the light of the world. A city set on a hill cannot be hidden. Nor do men light a lamp and put it under a peck measure, but on a lampstand, and it gives light to all in the house. Let your light so shine before men that they may see your moral excellence and your praiseworthy, noble, and good deeds and recognize and honor and praise and glorify your Father Who is in heaven. (Matthew 5:14-16 Amplified Bible)

Jesus taught that believers were light. Light speaks to us of the lifestyle of believers being a witness to the praiseworthiness of God's goodness. Our lives should dispel the darkness of evil and present the light of truth needful for those in darkness to find the door to salvation; that is, our lives should express personal faith in the Lord Jesus Christ. When the character of believers is marred by carnality, it is like putting the light "under a peck measure," or human sensuality. Carnality (immature Christian character) dims the light (our witness) and makes it very difficult for those in darkness to locate the door to salvation. There is no darkness (deception or falsity) in light because light (revelation of and from God) dispels darkness. In order for this truth to be every believer's reality, the lifestyle (witness) must be pure and not defiled by the carnality of the flesh: our opinions and dysfunctional emotions. When our lives are led by the Holy Spirit, our witness will shine revelation from God. In the Apostle Paul's letter to the church at Rome, we find some marvelous instructions on how to keep our Christian witness (light) pure and undefiled:

> I appeal to you therefore, brethren, and beg of you in view of [all] the mercies of God, to make a decisive dedication of your bodies [presenting all your members and faculties] as a living sacrifice, holy (devoted, consecrated) and well pleasing to God, which is your reasonable, rational, intelligent service and spiritual worship. Do not be conformed to this world (this age), [fashioned after and adapted to its external, superficial customs], but be transformed (changed) by the [entire] renewal of your mind [by its new ideals and its new attitude], so that you may prove [for yourselves] what is the good and acceptable and perfect will of God, even the thing which is good and acceptable and perfect [in His sight for you]. (Romans 12:1-2 Amplified Bible)

Being a child of God has a little more weight and responsibility to it than "getting our name in the Lamb's Book of Life and then waiting to go to heaven." All the children have a responsibility to surrender to the will of God for their lives and renew their minds with the Word of God while they are here in the earth realm. We are lights which are to reflect the truth—in the earth realm—about relationship with a loving Father through the redemptive work of Jesus Christ. Operating in anything other than the will of God for our lives will dim our light (witness) rendering us powerless to reflect the truth. Paul instructs believers to walk as children of the light:

> For once you were darkness, but now you are light in the Lord; walk as children of Light [lead the lives of those native-born to the Light]. For the fruit (the effect, the product) of the Light or the Spirit [consists] in every form of kindly goodness, uprightness of heart, and trueness of life. And try to learn [in your experience] what is pleasing to the Lord [let your lives be constant proofs of what is most acceptable to Him]. Take no part in and have no fellowship with the fruitless deeds and enterprises of darkness, but instead [let your lives be so in contrast as to] expose and reprove and convict them. (Ephesians 5:8-11 Amplified Bible)

In summary of Paul's instructions, we are to: (1) live the lifestyle of those native-born to the Light, (2) live in a manner that our lives cannot be labeled hypocrite, (3) know what manner of behavior pleases God and let our lives be a constant proof of that truth, and (4) stay away from anything that would dim our light (witness).

Once again, as sons of God, it is our duty to be salt and light in the earth realm. To gain practical insight into God's expectations of the performance of our duties, let us draw wisdom from the public ministry of Jesus Christ. Throughout Jesus public ministry, He was engaged in establishing the

Father's will in the earth realm by living in such a manner that His behavior was always well pleasing to the Father. Jesus operated in the earth as the Son of God-Son of Man with the anointing and the authority to administer and to establish the Kingdom of God in the earth. Jesus continuously demonstrated the duties of a Son by perpetuating the family's values and the Name of the Father in the earth. Demons recognized that He was the Son of God (Matthew 8:28-29), and people acknowledged Him as the Son of David (covenant man) having the authority to administer and establish the Kingdom of God in the earth (Mark 10:46-48). Believers, as sons of God, are to operate by the same anointing that was on Jesus to establish the Kingdom of God with power and authority in the earth realm.

Also, as we study the believers' responsibility as ambassadors of Christ, we gain insight into sonship duties. The Word of God teaches that believers are ambassadors of Christ (2 Corinthians 5:20). As ambassadors of the Kingdom of God, we are to consult and dispense whatever headquarters is mandating.

> We are Christ's ambassadors, and God is using us to speak to you. We urge you, as though Christ himself were here pleading with you, "Be reconciled to God!" (2 Corinthians 5:20 NLT)

Ambassadors represent the Kingdom which sent them. While ministering in the earth realm, Jesus represented the values of the Kingdom of God. As God's ambassador, Jesus said, "For I came down from heaven, not to do mine own will, but the will of him that sent me," (John 6:38). Hear the Son of God say, "For I have given unto them the words which thou gavest me; and they have received them, and they have believed that thou didst send me," (John 17:8). According to this verse, Jesus gave to others what the Father shared with Him in order to incite faith in the heart. As believers operate in the earth realm as ambassadors of the Kingdom of God, this same principle and attitude of mind which was in Christ Jesus is to be the heart attitude of every believer: give to others the words the Father has shared with you.

We are no longer slaves, but *sons of God* representing the Kingdom of God in the earth realm, so stay away from slave mentality and live bondage free. The Word of God says:

> And because ye are sons, God hath sent forth the Spirit of His Son into your hearts, crying, Abba, Father. Wherefore thou art no more a servant, but a son; and if a son, then an heir of God through Christ. But now, after that ye have known God, or rather are known of God, how turn ye again to the weak and beggarly elements, whereunto ye desire again to be in bondage? (Galatians 4:6-9)

Can we talk one-on-one for a moment? Listen. Don't allow your sonship experience to be clouded with the demands of opinions, emotionalism, or ritualism. Stay clear of these bondages and remember you are no longer obligated to cater to their demands—you are a son of God, an ambassador of the Kingdom of God.

As sons of God, believers are to count it a joyful but vital experience to be led by the wisdom and prompting of the Spirit of Truth, and not allow themselves to be pulled by worldly standards or opinions. The Apostle Paul states, "So we have stopped evaluating others by what the world thinks about them." (2 Corinthians 5:16a NLT) The sons of God should experience a transformation in thinking which transitions one to a higher plane of operating in this earth.

As we study the Written Word and allow the Holy Spirit to do surgery on our minds, this transformation and transition will take place. What an awesome fellowship we have to be in the presence of God the Holy Spirit and take to heart the counsel He offers. His presence and counsel prove that the sons of God are not orphans or slaves! The Holy Spirit's presence testifies that we are sons; we are ambassadors of the Kingdom of God!

In order to effectively operate as an ambassador perpetuating the family values and the Father's name in the earth, we will have to walk in sonship consciousness. Once again, we turn to our perfect example of one who walked in sonship consciousness and that is the Lord Jesus Christ.

> So Jesus answered them by saying, I assure you, most solemnly I tell you, the Son is able to do nothing of Himself (of His own accord); but He is able to do only what He sees the Father doing, for whatever the Father does is what the Son does in the same way [in His turn]. (John 5:19 Amplified Bible)

> So Jesus added, When you have lifted up the Son of Man [on the cross], you will realize (know, understand) that I am He [for Whom you look] and that I do nothing of Myself (of My own accord or on My own authority), but I say [exactly] what My Father has taught Me. And He Who sent Me is ever with Me; My Father has not left Me alone, for I always do what pleases Him. (John 8:28 & 29 Amplified Bible)

As the Spirit of Adoption trains believers to communicate with *"Abba, Father,"* our consciousness of His presence, and the truth that Jesus is alive, will increase. Let me take a side journey and explain an important biblical truth concerning the ministry of the Holy Spirit. If you notice, I have been using different names for the Holy Spirit; for example, Spirit of Adoption, Spirit of Truth, etc. Each of the names used represents an aspect of His ministry to the Church which is to be active in the life of every believer. Now, let us return to our study of being an ambassador in the Kingdom of God.

As ambassadors of the Kingdom, we are called to *reconcile, forgive, and intercede,* as we keep our hearts in tune with the Spirit of Adoption. Let's take a look at each of these dimensions of our calling:

1. *RECONCILE:* God is not angry with mankind, but as it is recorded in Romans 5:8, "But God shows and clearly proves His (own) love for us by the fact that while we were still sinners, Christ (the Messiah, the Anointed One) died for us." (Amplified Bible) Now, as sons of God, we have the privilege and authority to tell others that the case between sinners and God has been dismissed because of the work of Calvary. All that is needful now is that one believes that the work was accomplished for him/her personally. In short, personally believe that Jesus paid the penalty for your sins by using His own blood at Calvary. Now that is good news!

2. *FORGIVE:* Since sin has already been judged, we don't have to beat people across the head about sin, but tell them the way out: they need to repent and receive God's forgiveness. There is no need for penance, as some religions teach, because no one can pay for sins committed or earn forgiveness by doing good works. It took the cross of Jesus to remove sin and destroy its authority over our lives. The only thing needful is that we turn all the way from sin and receive God's forgiveness. Once forgiveness has set you free, stay

free and do not return to the bondage of sin again. In addition, free those who have trespassed against you by forgiving the offense. The Father's love and mercy extended toward us is one of our examples of how we are to forgive and extend mercy to others. God the Father loved us while we were seriously doing wrong and disobeying His commands. It was because of His great love that He sent Jesus to pay the price for our wrong doings. The forgiving spirit of Jesus is also an example of how we are to forgive others. After being beaten, spat on, and crucified for sins He never committed, from the cross, His voice cried out "Father forgive them for they know not what they do." We are recognized as sons of God because we are not like those who instigate evil and humiliate others. We are recognized as sons of God because we make and maintain harmonious relationships between God and man as well as man and man. As the Word of God says, "Blessed (enjoying enviable happiness, spiritually prosperous—with life-joy and satisfaction in God's favor and salvation, regardless of their outward conditions) are the makers and maintainers of peace, for they shall be called the sons of God!" (Matthew 5:9) As sons of God, our attitudes toward life are vastly different and unique from those walking in darkness who are not a part of the Kingdom of God. We bless and not curse, we rejoice in the Lord and not revile, that others might know that God's children are different from the children of the world. As children of God, we live by the Word of God which states, "But I say unto you, Love your enemies, bless them that curse you, do good to them that hate you, and pray for them which despitefully use you, and persecute you; That you may be the children of your Father which is in heaven: for he maketh his sun to rise on the evil and on the good, and sendeth rain on the just and on the unjust." (Matthew 5: 44-45)

3. *INTERCEDE:* Intercession gives believers the opportunity to acquire strategies on how to release the sound of heaven in the earth. Do not venture to exercise authority or power without first consulting God concerning the matter. As sons of God, we have a blood bought right to enter the Throne of Grace and talk with a loving *"Abba, Father"* face to face, that is, in open communication. As we abide by the instructions of the Holy Spirit, we too will be able to declare just as Jesus did, "repent for the kingdom of God is at hand." Once again, the effectiveness of intercession depends upon the willingness to receive instructions from the Holy Spirit and allow Him to assist with prayer.

## CHAPTER THIRTEEN

# THE VOICE OF SONSHIP

> You will also decide and decree a thing, and it
> will be established for you; And the light [of
> God's favor] will shine upon your ways. (Job
> 22:28 Amplified Bible)

The voice of sonship is released in the form of a decree.
What is a decree? According to Wycliffe Bible Dictionary,
decrees are "public proclamations, usually in writing, issued
by rulers to their subjects."[15] Decrees are authoritative,
powerful, and binding proclamations. The ruler's seat of
authority is the weight behind the decree. Thus, when a ruler
made a decree, unwavering obedience to that decree was
expected from the subjects under the authority of that ruler.

The earthly ministry of Jesus Christ is a demonstration
of how Kingdom decrees establish divine order—even to
the winds and waves obeying His voice. Since the earth was
created by God, it must respond to Kingdom decrees uttered
by those given His authority to declare them. Therefore, when
a Kingdom decree is issued by those in the legal position to
speak them, as Jesus was, any situation out of alignment with

---

15    Wycliffe Bible Dictionary, p. 446

Kingdom government must shift and come into alignment. Let's take a look at a passage that will give us insight into the authority of a kingly decree.

> For the word of a king is authoritative and powerful, And who will say to him, "What are you doing?" (Ecclesiastes 8:4 Amplified Bible)

> Since a king's word is supreme, who can say to him, "What are you doing?" (Ecclesiastes 8:4 NIV)

From this passage, in either translation, we learn that it is expected for kingly decrees to be obeyed and not questioned by those who are not in authority. Jesus fully expected for demons, sickness, and all the ills of the adversary, to obey His decrees. Even if demons questioned His purpose, they still obeyed His decree. Let us study an example:

> Just then a man in their synagogue who was possessed by an evil spirit cried out, "What do you want with us, Jesus of Nazareth? Have you come to destroy us? I know who you are— the Holy One of God!" "Be quiet!" said Jesus sternly. "Come out of him!" The evil spirit shook the man violently and came out of him with a shriek. The people were all so amazed that they asked each other, "What is this? A new teaching—and with authority! He even gives orders to evil spirits and they obey him." (Mark 1:26-27 NIV)

Once again, decrees are authoritative proclamations which are to be obeyed by those of lesser rank. As sons of God, given the legal right to exercise authority in the earth realm, we must always remember and rely on this foundational truth. The sons of God are in a higher rank than all the ills of the devil and we must expect for those ills to obey the Father's will decreed by us.

Jesus decreed the Father's authoritative plan for His life at the beginning of His earthly ministry:

> He went to Nazareth, where he had been brought up, and on the Sabbath day he went into the synagogue, as was his custom. And he stood up to read, Isaiah was handed to him. Unrolling it, he found the place where it is written: "The Spirit of the Lord is on me, because he has anointed me to preach good news to the poor. He has sent me to proclaim freedom for the prisoners and recovery of sight for the blind, to release the oppressed, to proclaim the year of the Lord's favor." (Luke 4:16-19, NIV)

This passage clearly gives us insight into the scope of Jesus' legal authority to decree the Father's will in the earth. It also gives us insight into His dependency on the presence of the Holy Spirit and the power of the anointing.

Multiple times in the Gospels, we find references to Jesus as the "Son of man," exercising authority to do the will of the Father in the earth (Matthew 13:41, Mark 13:26, Luke 12:8 and John 3:14). All that Jesus did aligned with God's spoken Word for operating as the Son of man anointed to exercise power in the earth. Before I venture further, let us establish a Scriptural foundation for the statement, "Son of man anointed to exercise power." The Bible teaches that Jesus operated in the earth realm by the power of the Holy Spirit and under the authority of Father God. There are two passages we can cross reference to view these truths: John 14:10 and Acts 10:38.

> Do you not believe that I am in the Father, and that the Father is in Me? What I am telling you I do not say on My own authority and of My own accord; but the Father Who lives continually in Me does the (His) works (His own miracles, deeds of power). (John 14:10 Amplified Bible)

> How God anointed and consecrated Jesus of Nazareth with the [Holy] Spirit and with strength and ability and power; how He went about doing good and, in particular, curing all who were harassed and oppressed by [the power of] the devil, for God was with Him. (Acts 10:38 Amplified Bible)

These two passages show the blueprint for how the household of faith is to reflect the Father's image in the earth realm: believers are to operate by the anointing as they seek to do the will of the Father in the earth realm. Believers are to stay away from speaking their own opinions or making things happen by their own strength.

Most of the time, when Jesus referred to Himself, He used the phrase "Son of man." This title can be viewed as both relational and prophetic. As a relational title, it brings into view the Incarnation (John 1:14). In no way does this title deny the deity of Christ, but it speaks to us of His humanity which gave Him the legal right to become our Kinsman-Redeemer (Leviticus 25:25-26, 48-49; Ruth 2:20). Because the children had bodies of flesh, He too had to take on a human body in order to redeem us. The title, "Son of man," is also prophetic in as much as it speaks of the Exalted One who will set up His

Kingdom reign on earth (Daniel 7:13-14). Now, let us move back into our study on the voice of sonship.

The Bible tells us that Jesus went about preaching, teaching, and healing all that were oppressed of the devil (Matthew 9:35, Acts 10:38). These acts He performed in alignment with God's original mandate for humankind to have dominion in the earth. Adam was God's son and legal representative in the earth. God's original plan was for the earth to recognize and yield to the voice of humankind operating as God's legal representative in the earth. Sin marred that original plan and God subjected the earth to bondage for fallen mankind's sake.

> For the creation (nature) was subjected to frailty (to futility, condemned to frustration), not because of some intentional fault on its part, but by the will of Him Who so subjected it—[yet] with the hope that nature (creation) itself will be set free from its bondage to decay and corruption [and gain an entrance] into the glorious freedom of God's children. (Romans 8:20-21 Amplified Bible)

The voice of sonship is one which echoes and perpetuates Kingdom authority in the earth: it shifts situations in the earthly realm to align with God's government. Once again, from the study of Jesus' earthly ministry, we gain understanding into how He perpetuated the Father's will in the earth through decrees (legal proclamations of authority that were to be obeyed). The decrees spoken by Jesus established salvation, deliverance, healing, forgiveness, and prosperity in the lives of the recipients of those decrees. The Word of God says that "All the people were amazed and said to each other, "What is this teaching? With authority and power he gives orders to evil spirits and they come out!" (Luke 4:36 NIV)

Jesus decreed that His church would operate with the voice of Kingdom authority in the earth, which is the voice of sonship:

> I will build my church, and the gates of hell shall not prevail against it. And I will give unto thee the keys of the kingdom of heaven: and whatsoever thou shall bind on earth shall be bound in heaven: and whatsoever thou shalt loose on earth shall be loosed in heaven, (Matthew 16:18-19).

As sons of God, our legal right to speak the Kingdom's decrees in the earth is one of the *keys of the kingdom of heaven"* which has the authority to bind and to loose. When believers truly understand the authority which God has given to us as sons of God, we will speak (decree) God's will in the earth and situations will shift and align themselves with Kingdom government. The earth must respond to the authoritative voice of the sons of God—those with the legal right to exercise Kingdom authority as they are led by the Holy Spirit. Sometimes manifestation is immediate, and at other times it is progressive. Nevertheless, the earth must obey the voice of the sons of God—those in the legal position to exercise Kingdom rulership (dominion) in the earth.

Believers, as joint heirs in the Kingdom, may exercise the same authority Jesus operated in during His earthly ministry. As joint heirs, whatever belongs to Jesus also belongs to us, which would include the legal right to operate in authority and power in the earth realm. For it is written that, "The Spirit himself testifies with our spirit that we are God's children. Now if we are children, then we are heirs—heirs of God and co-heirs with Christ, if indeed we share in his sufferings in order that we may also share in his glory." (Romans 8:16-17) The goal of Jesus' sufferings was to operate in complete obedience to the Father's will unhindered—even to death on the cross. In addition, we see another clear picture of the depth of Jesus' obedience as we visit the Garden of Gethsemane: "My Father, if it is not possible for this cup to be taken away unless I drink it, may your will be done," (Matthew 26: 42b NIV). The Book of Hebrews gives us a further description of this event: "During the days of Jesus' life on earth, he offered up prayers and petitions with loud cries and tears to the one who could save him from death, and he was heard because of his reverent submission." (5:7 NIV)

The goal of the sons of God should always be to operate in complete obedience (reverent submission) to the will of the Father. Why? When we truly understand that decrees are legal binding proclamations, and that the power and authority behind Kingdom decrees is the very throne of God, we will not want to decree anything that does not align with the Father's will or anything that will bring shame to our family name.

In our position as sons of God, we have returned to God's original decree for how mankind is to operate in the earth—with dominion (legal authority to exercise power). As believers in the redemptive work of Jesus Christ, we now have the right to reverently submit to our Father's will and exercise legal authority in the earth, and expect results. Where does one find the will of the Father? The will of the Father can plainly be seen in the Gospel of Jesus Christ. As we study the written Word and allow the Holy Spirit to direct our actions, He will impress upon our hearts the Father's will. As believers, we have the legal right to *degree our Father's will* in the earth and expect for His will to manifest as spoken.

## CHAPTER FOURTEEN

# STEWARDSHIP OF THE INHERITANCE

As every man hath received the gift, even so minister the same one to another, as good stewards of the manifold grace of God. (1 Peter 4:10)

According to this verse, believers are expected to be good stewards of the multi-faceted ability of grace and not hinder its work. Grace is God's ability at work imparting gifts to His people: salvation, empowerment, healing, protection, and the like. Once the knowledge of the ability of grace has been obtained, believers are not to obstinately reject any of God's gracious gifts. Believers are to receive all grace offers and not be indifferent toward the power of grace flowing from the redemptive work of Jesus. Divine gifts are not for picking and choosing, but for receiving.

The capacity and ability to function as sons of God in the earth realm started with faith working through grace and must continue in that same manner. In the faith working through grace experience, believers are to receive all that the redemptive work of Jesus Christ has to offer, which includes wholeness for the entire spirit, soul, and body. In the initial stage of union with Christ (new birth), every believer received, by faith working through grace, the gift of righteousness and should have, with great gratitude for the work of the cross, moved forward to Pentecost; that is, to receive the gift of the baptism in the Holy Spirit, even as the Early Church fathers were commanded to do.

> But you will receive power when the Holy Spirit comes on you; and you will be my witnesses in Jerusalem, and in all Judea and Samaria, and to the ends of the earth. (Acts 1:9 NIV)

Believers are to receive the gracious gift of the baptism of the Holy Spirit for the empowerment needful to operate in effective service in the Kingdom of God. Keep in mind that faith works through grace and that faith working through grace is the believer's lifestyle.

In addition to receiving empowerment as an active part of our good stewardship of the manifold grace of God, believers are to obey the wisdom of the Holy Spirit. The gift of salvation working in us was not wrought by any work of the flesh; neither can we continue the stewardship of that gift apart from the wisdom of the Spirit. Since all the gifts received from God are new terrain for every believer, believers will definitely need to receive God's wisdom in order to effectively operate in them. God's wisdom enlightens the heart with the understanding of what we have and how it is to function. Believers may acquire wisdom from two sources: the written Word of God and the guidance of the Holy Spirit. Neither of these sources will ever contradict one another. Thus, believers should make every effort to read the Word of God and listen for the wisdom of the Spirit in order to avoid falling prey to false interpretation and application of the written Word: Read, listen, and obey!

The exercise of good stewardship requires believers to mature in godly character. The word, *mature,* is not a reference to physical age, but to the progressive development of character. Father God expects for His children to grow in godly character which helps them to be good stewards of the family's inheritance. Immature sons do not position the heart to receive fresh revelation from God; therefore, are susceptible to false doctrine, the misappropriation of the family's inheritance, and inappropriate behavior which causes the family's name to be profaned. There are several passages which support these truths:

> However, brethren, I could not talk to you as to spiritual [men], but as to nonspiritual [men of the flesh, in whom the carnal nature predominates], as to mere infants [in the new life] in Christ [unable to talk yet!]. (1 Corinthians 3:1 Amplified Bible)

From this passage, we get a glimpse of the expectancy of growth in character which stems from new life in Christ. The word, *infants,* comes from the Greek word *nēpiŏs* meaning "simple-minded person, an immature Christian."[16] Because these believers had not developed maturity of character, they were unable to receive the revelations needful to help them represent the Kingdom of God before men. Instead of the fruit of the spirit actively working in their lives, they were "under the control of ordinary impulses," involved in envying, jealousy, wrangling, and factions. Let's take a look at another passage regarding immaturity.

---

[16] Strong's Exhaustive Concordance, #3516

Concerning this we have much to say which is hard to explain, since you have become dull in your [spiritual] hearing and sluggish [even slothful in achieving spiritual insight]. For even though by this time you ought to be teaching others, you actually need someone to teach you over again the very first principles of God's Word. You have come to need milk, not solid food. For everyone who continues to feed on milk is obviously inexperienced and unskilled in the doctrine of righteousness (of conformity to the divine will in purpose, thought, and action), for he is a mere infant [not able to talk yet]! But solid food is for full-grown men, for those whose senses and mental faculties are trained by practice to discriminate and distinguish between what is morally good and noble and what is evil and contrary either to divine or human law. (Hebrews 5:11-14 Amplified Bible)

These Christians had become "inexperienced and unskilled in the doctrine of righteousness," consequently, were not in position to represent the family's values or the Father's name in the earth realm. The sad implication in this passage is that the lack of their spiritual growth led to spiritual digression and a deficiency of godly character in their lives. Learn this spiritual lesson: where there is no spiritual progression, spiritual digression is inevitable.

Now, notice the statement, "...for those whose senses and mental faculties are trained by practice to discriminate and distinguish between what is morally good and noble and what is evil and contrary..." because there is also a lesson in its content. From this statement, we understand that maturity does not come by osmosis, but by training the senses and faculties to distinguish between good and evil. Although believers have been placed in the Body of Christ at the adult sonship level, that placement does not negate the truth that spiritual maturity comes through training the senses and faculties to discriminate and distinguish between what is morally good and what is evil. In the natural, whenever an individual is placed in a grade at school, that individual has to make a diligent effort to learn the course material for that grade; that is, of course, if the plan is to derive benefits from being in that grade. Likewise, in the Kingdom of God, every believer has to make a diligent effort to learn what it means to be a son of God, if they plan to derive benefits from and be a blessing in the Kingdom of God.

In view of the truth that believers live by every word which proceeds from the mouth of God, Romans 8:14 gives us the key to the spiritual application needful to train one how to mature as a son of God.

> For all who are led by the Spirit of God are sons of God. (Amplified Bible)

The Kingdom of God is new terrain for every believer; thus, seeking wisdom from the Holy Spirit for the practical application of the Word of God is not optional. Allowing the Holy Spirit the opportunity to teach, train, and guide our lives is a part of our ability to mature in godly character. There are four passages in the Book of John which detail how vital the ministry of the Holy Spirit is to believers.

> And I will ask the Father, and He will give you another Comforter (Counselor, Helper, Intercessor, Advocate, Strengthener, and Standby), that He may remain with you

141

forever—The Spirit of Truth, Whom the world cannot receive (welcome, take to its heart), because it does not see Him or know and recognize him. But you know and recognize Him, for He lives with you [constantly] and will be in you. (John 14:16-17 Amplified Bible)

But the Comforter (Counselor, Helper, Intercessor, Advocate, Strengthener, Standby), the Holy Spirit, Whom the Father will send in My name (in My place, to represent Me and act on My behalf], He will teach you all things. And He will cause you to recall (will remind you of, bring to your remembrance) everything I have told you. (John 14:26 Amplified Bible)

But when the Comforter (Counselor, Helper, Advocate, Intercessor, Strengthener, Standby) comes, Whom I will send to you from the Father, the Spirit of Truth Who comes (proceeds) from the Father, He [Himself] will testify regarding Me. (John 15:26 Amplified Bible)

But when He, the Spirit of Truth (the Truth-giving Spirit) comes, He will guide you into all the Truth (the whole, full Truth). For He will not speak His own message [on His own authority]; but He will tell whatever He hears [from the Father; He will give the message that has been given to Him], and He will announce and declare to you the things that are to come [that will happen in the future]. (John 16:13 Amplified Bible)

Every believer's dependency on the ministry of the Holy Spirit was never optional. I challenge you to study these passages and allow the Holy Spirit to make them a reality in your life.

Once again, Jesus is our example of walking as a matured son of God—one led by the Spirit of God. The Book of Matthew records a statement concerning Jesus that we should consider in our study of maturing sons.

> But the men marveled, saying, What manner
> of man is this, that even the winds and the sea
> obey him! (Matthew 8:27)

Believers should always have the answer to that question fully activated in the heart. Pacetti writes, "I will tell you what manner of man this is; He is a son of God, filled with the Holy Spirit and power,"[17]

The matured sons of God have learned how to walk in two realms: heaven and earth. They have deliberately shifted their affections heavenly, learned how to allow the love of God to motivate the heart, and seek only to do the will of God in the earth realm. In this manner, the family's values and the name of Jesus can be reflected in the earth through their obedient lives.

The matured sons of God have learned to live from the new nature within by their obedience to the prompting of the Holy Spirit. The matured sons of God yield their hearts to be motivated by the ministry of the Holy Spirit (the Spirit of Adoption) as He teaches them to observe the Father's heart from the new position of sonship. Consequently, their actions are perfectly aligned with Kingdom government and authority. Believers are not to be like the elder brother in Luke

---

[17]    Sozo: What It Means To Be Saved, p. 33

15:25-29, who failed to experience the benefit of being his father's son because his heart was stuck in works mentality. God has called believers to the position of sonship whereby they communicate, not from works mentality, but from a heart to heart child-like position with *"Abba, Father."*

The matured sons of God are not confused about the need for continuous intimate fellowship. They understand that fellowship with God is the source from which all Christian duties flow to others. Fellowship is the "fill-up" station and supply line believers are to partake of daily. Abiding in Jesus, the Living Vine, is not optional, but the life-line of spiritual nourishment needful to continue toward reaching the full maturity of character found in Him (Ephesians 4:13).

In retrospect of the teachings on the lifestyle of Jesus, He stands as our example of a matured son of God operating in priestly and kingly authority in the earth, and He is expecting for the Church to follow His example. His expectations of the Church operating in authority in the earth is evident in the statement, "the works that I do you will do and greater works than these because I go to the Father." (John 14:12, paraphrased)

Good stewardship of the inheritance is not optional. In Christianity, there are divine principles governing the stewardship of the family's name which believers are to obey: binding and loosing, honoring and not profaning, and demonstrating the power of the name of Jesus. Let us take a look at the Scriptural evidence of these divine principles.

> ➤ **BINDING AND LOOSING:** "And I will give unto thee the keys of the kingdom of heaven: and whatsoever thou shall bind on earth shall be bound in heaven: and whatsoever thou shalt loose on earth shall be loosed in heaven." (Matthew 16:19) Jesus gave this promise after Peter operated in the revelation that He was the

Messiah, the Son of God (Matthew 16:16). This verse implies that operating in the revelation of Jesus being the Messiah, the Son of the Living God, gives us the authority to bind the activities of the enemy in the earth realm and establish Kingdom order in places that are occupied by the enemy. Now, understand that operating in the revelation that Jesus is the Christ (Messiah) the Son of God opens the heart to receive instructions in regard to His redemptive work. It is the revelation that Jesus is the Messiah (the One God sent to redeem mankind from sin and restore things back to divine order) that is the *key* to operating in authority in the earth realm.

➢ **HONORING AND NOT PROFANING:** "I therefore, the prisoner of the Lord, beseech you that you walk worthy of the vocation wherewith ye are called, with all lowliness and meekness, with longsuffering, forbearing one another in love; endeavouring to keep the unity of the Spirit in the bond of peace." (Ephesians 4:1-3) This passage of Scripture implies that believers are not to seek a reputation for self, especially not at the expense of sacrificing the unity of the Spirit and the bond of peace that identifies us as children of God. As well beloved children, we are to honor our heavenly Father and not profane our family's name by engaging in irreverent behavior.

➢ **DEMONSTRATING THE POWER:** "Verily, verily, I say unto you, He that believeth on me, the works that I do shall he do also; and greater works than these shall he do; because I go unto my Father. And whatsoever ye shall ask in my name, that will I do, that the Father may be glorified in the Son." (John 14:12-13) This verse implies that in order to demonstrate the power of the Name of Jesus, one must believe on Jesus; that

145

is, trust in, rely on, and have confidence in the person of the Lord Jesus Christ. According to Ephesians 2:10, believers are God's workmanship "created in Christ Jesus unto good works which God hath before ordained that we should walk in them." Therefore, as sons of God, our work has already been established and is to be accomplished by demonstrating the power of the Name of Jesus.

Intercession is one of the methods believers employ in stewardship of the inheritance and a wonderful way to reflect God's image in the earth. Through intercession, believers perpetuate the Father's Name in the earth and distribute the family's values in the spiritual realm for manifestation in the earth. As sons of God, intercession is to be at an intimate level of communication that is free of orphan mentality. Matured sons of God enter into intercession with the full understanding and assurance that God is *"Abba Daddy,"* who loves us and whom we love. Maturing sons of God have cast the care of self upon Jesus and are available to intercede for others.

Always remember that New Testament intercession is about fellowship with God at the level of sonship, understanding the responsibilities of an offspring in the Kingdom of God and exercising the stewardship of those responsibilities in the earth. As stewards of the family's name, sons of God seek to respect and uplift the integrity of the name of Jesus in every area of life. According to the Amplified Version of Philippians 2:12, there is a self-distrust that every believer should allow to motivate the heart in order to move away from anything which might bring a blemish to, or cause others to profane, the name of Jesus Christ.

Therefore, my dear ones, as you have always obeyed [my suggestions], so now, not only [with the enthusiasm you would show] in my presence but much more because I am absent, work out (cultivate, carry out to the goal, and fully complete) your own salvation with reverence and awe and trembling (self-distrust, with serious caution, tenderness of conscience, watchfulness against temptation, timidly shrinking from whatever might offend God and discredit the name of Christ).

As members of the family of God, believers are to willingly "with serious caution" make every effort to reflect the accurate value system of the family. We are to move away from anything which would cause a warped image of God or the Kingdom of God in the minds of those observing our lives. God's love for people is great, and as sons of God, we want to accurately reflect that message in the earth realm.

# RESOURCE AND BIBLIOGRAPHY

Holy Bible: King James Version, Thomas Nelson Publisher, Nashville, Tennessee, 1989.

Holy Bible: New Living Translation, TouchPoint Bible, Tyndale House Publishers, Incorporated, Wheaton, Illinois, 1996.

Holy Bible: The Everyday Life Bible Amplified Version, Warner Faith, New York, New York, 2006 by Joyce Meyer.

Holy Bible: The Thompson Chain-Reference Bible, New International Version, B. B. Kirkbride Bible Company, Incorporated, Indianapolis, Indiana, 1990.

Holy Bible: The Word In Life Study Bible, New King James Version, Thomas Nelson Publishers, Nashville, Tennessee, 1996.

Kenyon, E. W., *New Kind of Love (The)*, Kenyon Gospel Publishing Society, Lynnwood, Wyoming.

Knight, George R., *Walking With Paul Through The Book of Romans*, Daily Devotional for Adults, Review and Herald Publishing Association, 2002.

Long, Ednorleatha, *Reflecting God's Image*, Good News Publications, East St. Louis, Illinois, 2013.

Long, Ednorleatha, *Sonship*, Good News Publication, East St. Louis, Illinois, 2012.

McClain, Alva J., *Romans: The Gospel of God's Grace*, BMH Books, Winona Lake, Indiana, 1973.

Pacetti, David, *Sozo: What It Means To Be Saved*, Albury Press, Tulsa, Oklahoma, 1985.

Piper, John, Why is Jesus Called "Son of Man"? Desiring God @ http://www.desiringgod.org/interviews/why-is-jesus-called-son-of-man

Strong, James, Strong's Exhaustive Concordance of the Bible, Hendrickson Publishers, Peabody, Massachusetts.

Webster's Seventh New Collegiate Dictionary, G. & C. Merriam Company Publishers, Springfield, Massachusetts, 1961.

Wycliffe Bible Dictionary, Charles F. Pfeiffer, Howard F. Vos, John Rea, Editors, Hendrickson Publishers, Peabody, Massachusetts, 1975.

# ABOUT THE AUTHOR

Ednorleatha Long, seminar leader, conference host, author, and teacher, is an avid student of the Word of God. Her heart's desire is to see believers grow in the grace and knowledge of our Lord and Savior Jesus Christ.

In 1984, after what she refers to as a "Damascus Road Experience" with the Lord, Ednorleatha received the baptism of the Holy Spirit which empowered her for Kingdom service.

She is the founder and administrator of the Ministry Preparatory Training School where she continues to train many five-fold ministry gifts from the Illinois-Missouri bi-state area.

Ednorleatha is also the founder and senior pastor of the Christian Growth Center Church located in East St. Louis, Illinois. Her continuous personal fellowship with the Lord empowers her gifts for ministering toward the building up of the Body of Christ.

Ednorleatha received a Bachelor of Arts in Biblical Studies from the Christian Bible College and Seminary; Master of Ministry, Doctorate of Biblical Studies, and Doctorate of Theology degrees from the International College of Bible Theology.